APPROACHING INFINITY

APPROACHING INFINITY

∞

A Practical Workbook to Help Us Achieve Our Goals in Life

David A. Waples

iUniverse, Inc.

New York Lincoln Shanghai

APPROACHING INFINITY
A Practical Workbook to Help Us Achieve Our Goals in Life

iUniverse, Inc.

For information address:
iUniverse, Inc.
2021 Pine Lake Road, Suite 100
Lincoln, NE 68512
www.iuniverse.com

ISBN: 0-595-33147-5

Printed in the United States of America

For my children

Contents

Preface

...faith without works is dead...—James 2:26

The strategy and techniques outlined in this workbook, *if applied with true passion and commitment*, can revolutionize how you think about the purpose of your life and what you can accomplish during it. For the first thirty-five years of *my* life, I felt like the subject of the Groucho Marx quip, "I've worked my way up from nothing to a state of extreme poverty." But, once I applied the simple strategy of *Approaching Infinity*—goal-setting and life mission planning—I converted, almost magically, more dreams into reality, and experienced more health, wealth, and happiness in a few years than I did in the previous three-and-a-half decades.

The shelves in the bookstores and libraries are pregnant with self-help books, self-improvement tapes, and biographies of positive thinkers waiting to deliver the "good news" to us. All of these resources for improving our life have one thing in common—they are all good. Some are better than others are to be sure, and different approaches are more appropriate for the unique styles of distinct individuals. Still, all publications on these subjects are also remarkably similar in the mission to help us create positive change in our lives. The books, CDs, and tapes often claim this goal is much simpler than we imagine. It is *not* because the authors cannot think up new ideas. Rather, it *is* because the sound, fundamental principles of good living are incredibly basic and available to everyone. What else needs to be said then? If the guideposts on the road to success are so easily marked, why doesn't everyone see them along his or her travels in life? Why doesn't everyone follow them if they are so obvious? Why aren't there more happy people everywhere getting all they want out of life?

One likely answer is *balance*. While all of us are busy bellying up to the cafeteria of life precariously placing item after item on our flimsy tray, we find ourselves often trying to keep our selections from spilling to the floor before we make it to the table to gorge ourselves with our personal smorgasbord. Occasionally, an item tumbles from our tray, and in an effort to rescue the precious delicacy, the entire seven-course meal dives for the ground. The result of this action is embarrassment, a waste of time and money, and to add insult to injury, we are still very hungry.

Another possible reason is *control*. As the saying attributed to Mark Twain goes, "everybody talks about the weather, but nobody does anything about it." But unlike the weather, we do have control over our lives. However, many of those that tap such available resources do not follow through. Reading about goal achievement is not doing. That is why this book is different. *Approaching Infinity* is a *workbook* where you can, step by step, write down exciting, worthy goals and then map out a plan to achieve them right as you read along. *Approaching Infinity* is not a text to read, put on the shelf, and then collect dust. Studies show that most people retain only 50 percent of new material one day after reading it. For example, one study of students listening to material on which they knew there would be a test (a powerful motivator!) revealed that the students remembered only half the information.[1] After a few weeks, retention often shrinks to 10 percent or less! *Approaching Infinity* should be a constant companion to review what we want to do in life and remind ourselves of the effective techniques that can assist us in reaching our goals. It is not a book to be loaned to others—it is uniquely our own. It is incomplete without our active participation and needs to be read with a pencil or pen in hand. *Approaching Infinity* requires us to think, soul search, make tough choices, and come to difficult decisions. It can help us face our fears and find solutions to the obstacles in our life. It is most effective when we let our imagination fly and see visions of things that do not currently exist. As a result, we can convert what previously seemed impossible into reality.

Some people learn the lessons of goal-setting and successful living when they are children. Others absorb these strategies as a young adult. A significant number of adults adopt these skills only after a painful "mid-life" crisis, when the children go off to college, or when they realize that they have not come as far financially as they thought they would twenty years before. Unfortunately, a significant number of people arrive to the same conclusions about how they should live their lives while on their deathbed. One thing is for certain—we face the lessons of life daily and are forever committed to repeating the courses until we study and pass the tests. And despite the relief of completing each challenging exam, we then immediately proceed to the next lesson and commence the process anew.

No matter what stage of life, level of success, or status of happiness in which we currently find ourselves, the concepts outlined in *Approaching Infinity* can lead us to a never-ending and continually improving mode of living. By taking effective action, the result will enrich our personal, social, intellectual, physical, financial, and spiritual lives.

This book is structured with the metaphor of building a home. That is, our house of goals. Chapter One "The Light at the End of the Tunnel" questions the reality of how we live our lives and requires us to accept who is responsible for our current situation. Chapter Two "Reading the Obits" helps us to look at the current house in which we live—what we have accomplished in our lives so far—and questions whether we are satisfied with the results. Chapter Three "The House That Goals Built" examines the choices and decisions we must make in order to begin remodeling or constructing of our new house of goals. Chapter Four "A Solid Foundation" explains how to form a mission or "purpose" statement, which is a required stable foundation for our home. Chapter Five "Framing Our Home" discusses the importance of values and beliefs in our lives, the boards and nails that hold together our goal-setting structure. Chapter Six "Goals—The Blueprint for Action" describes why many people do not form goals, and helps us overcome the obstacles in order to devise a proper blueprint for our lives. Chapter Seven "Brainstormy Weather" discusses the brainstorming process, a creative way to set our minds afire with possibilities for the future. Chapter Eight "The Goal Litmus Test" makes sure we double-check our proposed goals to see if they are right for us. Chapter Nine "The Six-Step Goal-Setting Action Plan" is a structured guide to properly chart our strategy for building our strong house of goals. Chapter Ten "The Goal Motivation Wheel" reveals the most effective way to take the first step in the daunting task of constructing our dream home. Chapter Eleven "Goal "DOERS" Winning Qualities" depicts essential attitudes and actions that will determine our ultimate outcome. And Chapter Twelve "The ABC Strategies of Success" reveals twenty-six qualities that will insure we build an edifice worthy of our purpose and keep our new home in peak condition. At the back of the book is an *Approaching Infinity* Goals Checklist we can photocopy to map out all of our goals and strategies to achieve them.

Let's commence the voyage. As the Chinese proverb states, "The longest journey begins with just a single step." Our first step on the *Approaching Infinity* road requires us to break old barriers.

Introduction:
Easy Barrier Breakers

To see the world in a grain of sand
And a heaven in a wild flower,
Hold infinity in the palm of your hand
And eternity in an hour.—William Blake

What is "Infinity?" Mathematically, infinity (represented by the Greek letter ∞) is defined as a number larger than any given number or values. According to my understanding of the laws of physics, (apologies to Albert Einstein and Steven Hawking), we cannot reach infinity. Not the fastest rocket ship can propel us there. And, no matter how much we move toward this unreachable point, it will still be equally far away from us. What does that mean to our life? What has it meant for others? For example:

- Steel-magnate Andrew Carnegie was a very rich man. But, he donated millions to his charitable foundation. If he retained all of his money for himself and invested it, he could have been richer.

- Baseball home-run king Hank Aaron hit 755 home runs in his career in the National League, more than any other player in American baseball history. But what if he could have filled the designated-hitter role later employed by the American League? Given a few more seasons, he could of hit more round-trippers.

- Mathematical genius Albert Einstein is the quintessential figure of human intelligence. However, many scientists say we—even the Einsteins among us—only use a fraction of our brain capacity. Therefore, Einstein may have been smarter if he could have maximized the use of his gray matter.

The point is that no matter how much we expect to accomplish in a lifetime, we can still enhance our earnings, improve our relationships, increase our knowledge, accomplish greater tasks, and achieve loftier goals than we previously believed. As we confidently move toward our chosen destination, we will make small steps at first, but after a while, we may make giant leaps of progress. After concentrated effort, our growth and potential can expand geometrically to bounds that we previously thought impossible. However, there is a point of diminishing returns. More and more effort may achieve smaller and smaller gains as we reach the top percentile of our performance capability. Ask any Olympic athlete who wins a race by hundredths of a second. And, of course, no matter how far we go, we cannot truly touch infinity. But, the secret is, we do not have to. It is not *where we finish*, but rather, *how we pursue* our dreams that really matter.

Because we cannot be the "best" in everything, we often settle for being the "inferior" in many things. "Oh, I can't do that!" we proclaim when faced with a new challenge. As a result, we shy away from even trying the things that our heart secretly and passionately wants to attempt.

Approaching Infinity is about the *pursuit* of goals, not necessarily the glory of their attainment. It is about the thrill of the chase of excellence. It is the joyful experience of striving for accomplishment. Popular television ad slogans seem to sum it up simply. Nike told us, "Just Do It." A Nissan Motor Company ad advised, "Life is a Journey. Enjoy the Ride." Although television advertising may have few things that enlighten us, sometimes the simplest advice is the best.

"Nature is neutral; it doesn't care who wins."[2] So said Earl Nightingale, one of the grandfathers of the American personal development movement in the twentieth century. Who are the goal-achievers? President Ronald Reagan sounded the clarion call in his first inaugural address in 1981: "If not us, who? If not now, when?" If we can accept that as a premise, why not us? George Bernard Shaw wrote, "You see things; and you say why. I dream of things that never were; and I say, 'why not?'"

Those people who buy a lottery ticket with the fantasy of winning 50 million dollars in the big Powerball drawing rationalize spending their last buck saying, "Somebody's got to win, it might as well be me." But in real life, people do not reach enduring and true success in life by lottery drawing. But then again, everyone is eligible in the carousel of life to try to grab the brass ring. We cannot win, however, unless we play. It is time for us to get in the game. We are no longer in the stands, cheering on the players on the field. Go for it.

1

The Light at the End of the Tunnel

If you don't know where you are going, you might wind up someplace else.—Yogi Berra, (attributed)

Yogi [Lawrence Peter] Berra, the former baseball coach and Hall of Fame player known for his mixed up adages, was once asked what time is was. According to television and radio interviewer Larry King, Berra responded, "You mean now?"[3]

When is the best time to begin our journey to the center of our goals? Well, what time is it—now? The Chinese proverb rings true: "The best time to plant a tree was twenty years ago. The second best time is right now."

Many people drift through time allowing the wind and currents to carry them through the ocean of life. Others decide to set sail and take advantage of the wind and manage the current. They chart their course and venture toward their destination, compass in hand. One opportunity to make a life-changing decision to set sail rather than be blown adrift is when we get, as the television commentator in the film *Network* proclaimed, "mad as hell and not going to take it anymore."

Often, many of us feel trapped in a quagmire of onerous obligations, shattered dreams, and unfulfilled expectations. Many people feel this way even though we live in the most sovereign nation on earth, with more liberties and luxuries that could not be contemplated by our forefathers. Despite being the envy of impoverished and freedom-seeking people of the world, we sometimes feel ensnared in spite of our own liberty. Many of us are employed in jobs with earnings far exceeding our parents' incomes and living cellular-satellite-computer lifestyles they never fathomed. Yet, we wallow in the role of prisoner. Many of us feel jailed by bully employers, imprisoned in dead-end jobs, and subjugated by government without freedom of choice in our lives. We battle to make ends meet and struggle for a little breathing space. In other words, we feel cornered.

Despite our brand new automobiles with dual air bags and anti-lock brakes, some claim that our standard of living is declining. But widescreen TVs and DVD players, personal computers connected to the Internet, and cellular communication are within the reach of nearly every working person. Thirty years ago we would only see James Bond with such powerful accouterments. But we hear the gap between the rich and poor continues to widen. Still, we want more gadgets, feel indigent, and may be jealous of others with much more material wealth than we have. Nothing is ever enough because we are tied in the endless tangle of "more."

Despite surveys revealing how busy today's worker is, we possess more "free time" than any society ever known to mankind. Yet we feel rushed, never completing our tasks. Microwave dinners, fast-food drive-through restaurants, and automatic devices in our homes complete our ordinary tasks faster and more efficiently. Nevertheless, we often are unsuccessful in completing the most mundane tasks as we hoped. We find efficient is not necessary effective.

Many of us experienced a stable childhood, are blessed with healthy and relatively affluent families, and have few threats to our current relationships. But the quality of those relationships may not be as good as we would like them to be. When we talk to each other, what do we talk about? Even for those of us who "struggle" to meet the rent, the mortgage, or utility bills, how does our wealth compare to others in the world or our own ancestors? We are incredibly wealthy—at least materially. But we cannot place a monetary value on the quality of our personal relationships.

We know more about health and fitness than any preceding generation, and despite the warnings of consuming certain foods or engaging in unhealthy habits, we often choose to go down the unhealthy path. In the United States, adults are not forced to live a life of depravity through malnutrition. Recent studies show that the United States is the most overweight nation on earth. The journal *Science* predicts that 40 percent of the American public will be obese by 2006.[4] However, we find solutions around every corner. Low-fat ice cream. No-fat cake. Low-cholesterol eggs. Oat-bran muffins. Abmasters. Treadmills. Vitamin supplements. For very smoker who claims he or she cannot kick the habit, there are two or more that have. Still, too many Americans remain overweight, inactive, and generally ignorant of the consequences of their unhealthy habits. In other words, as a nation, we are fat, lazy, and often stupid. Our nation's enemies do not need chemical or biological weapons of mass destruction; we are smoking, eating, and lounging ourselves to death.

We are connected to more knowledge than any intellectual society in the history of the world. New libraries with thousands of volumes are free for anyone to use. Cable television offers hundreds of channels—some of which we can actually learn from. The worldwide web is virtually limitless. Audiobooks abound for those who do not have time to read. CD-ROMs possess information on how to learn to do anything. And despite the "crisis" in public education, do our children lack any opportunities compared to the starving youth in the Third World or Abraham Lincoln attending a one-room schoolhouse? And yet, standardized test scores remain stagnant for many of our children. A plethora of public colleges and state universities exist and numerous scholarships are available for those that aggressively seek them. But how many of us have pursued a higher degree with as much passion as we should? When is the last time we browsed through the public library, read a non-fiction book, or learned a new skill?

As great American writer-philosopher Henry David Thoreau wrote in his classic work *Walden*, "Many men live lives of quiet desperation." Though the hustle and bustle of nineteenth-century New England cannot hold a candle (no pun intended) to today's Boston traffic jam, Thoreau's words ring ever more true today. Many of us live an existence of "virtual loneliness"—home alone with a TV dinner watching re-runs of sit-coms—as a world of people eke out survival day to day, sorely in need of their neighbor's help. Many elderly are deserted by their children. Some children are abandoned by their parents—both literally and figuratively. The infirm are avoided by most. There are an unlimited number of causes, agencies, and nonprofit groups that need helping hands, and they continually ask for volunteers. Often, those calls go unheeded by the many who are qualified to assist. Instead, they sit on their hands, feeling sorry for themselves because of the emptiness of their own lives.

In 1997, President Bill Clinton, along with former presidents George Herbert Walker Bush and Jimmy Carter, led a new call to volunteerism. Some in the media reported on the idea of volunteerism as if it were a new and foreign concept. In reality, volunteerism is what makes our nation strong, vibrant, and compassionate. President George W. Bush repeated this call to service by urging Americans to pledge a significant amount of service hours during their lifetime. The horrific events of September 11, 2001, were a wake-up call for many that were consumed by their own petty problems. How can we be lonely when there are so many that are in true desperate need? Does this put our own situation into better perspective? Before setting sail on our ocean of dreams, we should discover how to want and appreciate what we already have, rather than lusting after what we do not have and think we need.

There are an infinite number of ways to improve the quality of our lives. I am writing this today to learn *with* you concerning some of those methods. I have all the answers…for me. But I do not have any solutions for you. You have them within yourself.

In other words, I've got good news and bad news. First, the bad news:

You are responsible for your current situation in life.

Next, the good news:

You are responsible for your future situation in life.

You have the power to make more money, if it is a worthy goal to help serve your true purpose. Your financial well-being is not solely up to the munificence of your employer. *You* have the ability to rise ahead within your current or any other organization. Your career development is not decided solely by the whims of your boss. *You* have the capability to increase the amount of love in your life. Love is not controlled by how others view you. *You* have the responsibility and the strength to improve your physical health and your energy level. Your physical state is not solely predetermined by your heredity. *You* have the capacity to enlarge the knowledge you possess. Knowledge and skill does not end at Freudian-determined childhood experiences. Many sociologists point out that the environment strongly shapes a person's abilities, wealth, education, or social status. There may be some merit to that argument. After all, as the computer axiom goes: garbage in—garbage out. Remember the cartoon character *Pogo* who said, "We have met the enemy, and they are us!" It is *us* that willingly input the garbage into our own programming.

The goal and success techniques discussed in this book are not earth-shattering or unique concepts. They are as old as the hills. But this book can be used as a new guide to actually apply them to our own lives and obtain results. Most of these thoughts can be implemented into our daily lives at little or no cost. Consultants market some of these suggestions for hundreds, even thousands of dollars. But they remain simple, timeless, and fresh mainly because they work! But all of these threads of success are utterly worthless unless we decide to weave them into the fabric of our lives.

If we make the decision to change our life to accept any of these recommendations, commit to them, and believe in them, we will be astounded at the power we have within us. The biggest question we have to answer first is "why?" *Why* do we want to make a change in our life? *Why* do we want to learn more? *Why* do we desire an increased income? *Why* do we want to lose weight? *Why* do we need to form better relationships?

How effective is goal-setting as described in *Approaching Infinity*? What is the significance of positive imaging? When should we commit to life planning? Why do we need to form a written statement of purpose? Does taking action on these items actually produce results?

The proof provided in the answers to these questions, as they say, is in the pudding. Take the following example:

In 1996, entertainer George Burns died at the age of ninety-nine, a few months shy of becoming a centenarian. His wife, Gracie, passed away in the 1950s. For many people, the death of a loved one often signals a death sentence for oneself. Statistics show that an astounding number of surviving spouses die within five years of the death of their husband or wife, even at relatively early ages. A considerable number of people pass away within two years. What made George Burns live more than forty-years longer than his wife? Was it daily use of cigars? An occasional scotch and soda?

George Burns booked the London Palladium for his 100th-birthday party while he was in his eighties. After his seventieth birthday, his most famous movie roles evolved. For goodness sakes, the man was the only person to play God in a movie and get away with it. He wrote a book titled "How to Live to Be 100 or More." If you followed the career of George Burns in any way, was there ever a doubt in your mind that he really was going to live to be 100 or more? Well, he came close.

In his last book, Burns wrote, "When the Man knocks on your door, you have to go. When He knocks on my door, I'm not opening it. I'm going to stay in show business until I'm the only one left." When the ninety-year-old plus comedian fell in the bathtub and cracked his head open he said, "Things haven't been the same since. Well, the bathtub is the same. But I'm not. That doesn't mean I'm giving up. Far from it. I'm still an optimist. But I'm not stupid. That nurse isn't watching me all day to see if my toupee is on straight."[5]

How did he manage to live to be nearly 100 years old? I believe it was because he expected to. He had a plan. He had a goal. He was *Approaching Infinity*. He positively envisioned he would live an entire century. He filled his years with service to others through his God-given talent, and most important, he knew how to delight in the trip. Can anyone live to be 100 years old just because he or she expects to? Maybe not. But we can all expect to feel joy in the journey no matter how long it is.

How many of us are just sitting out this glorious train ride here on earth? Are we waiting to arrive at an undefined mysterious destination that will magically fulfill our dreams and give purpose to our life? Do we feel in control of our destination? Do we look out the window of this rail car of life and only watch the poignant scenery of other people's exciting lives through our television screens? Are we living the life that someone else, perhaps a parent or a spouse, carved out for us? Do we define our daily existence as merely a bit player with others in the lead role? Are we living our life solely to benefit our children? Are we living our life vicariously through our kids, pressuring them to achieve the aims that we could not? Are we satisfied with our lives? Are we content with our accomplishments? Have we discovered our true purpose in life? Will I ever stop asking these tough questions?

All right, already! I raise these issues not to make us depressed, though we often do not have answers that fill us with total satisfaction. Rather, these are questions we sometimes refuse to ask ourselves because we fear the answers. Also, the questions posed here are not profound. We probably make these inquiries of ourselves at various points of our life. One thing is for certain. No matter how long we have been traveling life's uncertain railway, the answers to the questions are never easy. But we have within ourselves the capability to choose our destination, lay down our own track of goals, and relish the adventure.

Before we map out any changes in the direction of our lives, it is always best to take out a compass and find out where we stand. How far have we come? What direction are we headed? Are we on target or are we desperately lost? Do we even have a compass? Most important, let's decide whether we are fulfilled with our experiences so far. And if not, what mid-course corrections can we make? We are not sentenced to travel on the tracks someone else or our own fears laid for us. It is time to jump the track and chart our own passage.

The next chapter will help us determine how to take an inventory of where we are on the railway of life.

2

Reading the Obits—Where Are We Now?

The report of my death was an exaggeration.—Mark Twain

Imagine waking up tomorrow morning, donning your terry-cloth bathrobe, and retrieving an errant-thrown newspaper from the steps of your front porch. You walk back into the house, fix a double-dose caffeine expresso, and sit down at the kitchen table, preparing to slap some strawberry jam on a bagel. You open up the newspaper the newsboy folded into a makeshift football, and brush off the dirt and dew that the projectile publication absorbed during its roll on the front lawn. Glancing at the morning's headlines, you begin a search inside the paper for something that is a little less depressing than the famine in an obscure nation, the latest gloomy economic figures, or the search for bodies in last week's plane crash. As you probe deeper into the journal fingering through the fresh ink-stained pages, you do a double-take. You thought you saw something familiar. You turn back a page, frustrated as the cut pages stick together. You open to the obituaries. You see a picture of someone who looks exactly like you. After you rub your eyes, you take a second look. It is you.

Next to your picture is your obituary, prepared by a new college intern at the local newspaper as her first assignment. The article begins,

"Suddenly, on Wednesday,..." then your name, misspelled, shouts at you in bold print. You read on. All the words are only vaguely familiar. They are bland, uninteresting, and robotic. You continue, still with interest, looking for a tribute to your life that could be a best-selling biography. But what you read sounds as exciting as a recipe for corn-bread muffins. A line of sweat forms on your forehead; your blood pumps at a rapid pace. You are getting nervous, scared, worried, shocked, irritated, frustrated, and angry—downright furious.

Are you enraged because you realize you are dead, deceased, food for worms, pushing up daisies, gone to meet your maker? No, of course not. You are incensed with these measly three paragraphs that sum up your life, your contribution to society—your legacy. And to top it off, they misspelled your name!

Does this scenario sound far-fetched? It is not. In fact, it happened to a Swedish chemist and inventor. He worked to develop mines, torpe-does, and other explosives. In 1867, he achieved his goal by reducing the volatility of nitroglycerin. He called his invention "dynamite." One morning, he opened up the newspaper and read his obituary. The head-line read something like: "Inventor of Dynamite Dies." In fact, it was a younger brother who died in an explosion while developing the volatile materials. The chemist determined that his life must have more mean-ing than inventing devices that very often killed people. So, he decided, after a lifetime of inventing, to change the direction of the course of his life. His will provided that the major portion of his $9 million estate be set up as a fund to establish yearly prizes for merit in physics, chemistry, medicine and physiology, literature, and world peace. His name was Alfred Bernhard Nobel. Have you ever heard of the Nobel Peace Prize?

What made Charles Dickens' "Ebeneezer Scrooge" make an about-face and decide to alter his attitude and his life's purpose? Was it just death? Or was it more than that? Was it the Ghost of Christmas Past, who showed him the fact that he had once loved and forgotten the wonderful feeling of a warm heart? Was it the Ghost of Christmas Present that revealed that Scrooge had the power to affect other's lives in a positive way through the gift of his service and abundance or in a negative way with his miserliness? Or was it the Ghost of Christmas Future's premonition that no one would miss him when he was gone? It was all of these.

People that survive heart attacks or serious accidents often shift gears abruptly and begin a transformation of how they take care of their physical bodies as well as how they treat their family and friends. Those who have been on the brink of death often adopt a radically different outlook on life once they realize how close to the grave they were. Many say, as President Ronald Reagan did as he brushed with death after a 1981 assassination attempt, that the rest of their lives are "on God" since only He pulled them back from certain death.

As Elisabeth Kübler-Ross taught us in her ground-breaking book *On Death and Dying*, people near the end of their lives do not fear death. Rather, they fear *not having lived.* Conversely, even those who have lived full, abundant lives often want to squeeze more out of life because they believe they can contribute more to others. One of the most prolific writers in the twentieth century, the late Isaac Asimov—author of hundreds of books on science fact and science fiction—was once asked what he would do if he knew he only had a few months to live. Asimov responded, "I'd type faster."

Sharon, a thirty-eight-year-old mother with ovarian cancer said this: "What bothers me is not that I might die, but that I never really got to live my life. Having cancer has taught me to take charge of my decisions and to feel powerful. I want to know how to use this power in my daily life and not slip back into my old feelings of depression and lack of confidence. I want so much to live my life even if it is only for a few more months or years."[6]

Facing death square in the face might be a bit too morbid for some of us. Well, let's try another one. Imagine that you are seventy-five years old (for some of us couch potatoes, it will not be too difficult) and are seated at the head table of a testimonial dinner that is being held in your honor. This tribute is being held to salute everything that you have accomplished in your life, the many people you have touched, and the metaphoric mountains you have climbed. In attendance is everyone you have ever known and everyone you wish you knew. A small piece of paper is clenched in your hands with remarks you will make when called to the podium. But you are not concerned with that. What you really are interested in is the musical sound of your own name as various speakers talk about you. You sit at the table, adjust your hearing aid, and listen to the master of ceremonies as she begins a long list of accolades and accomplished feats noted by the meaningful people in your life that you have helped. What will the emcee say about you?

OPPORTUNITY:

If your obituary were to appear in <u>tomorrow morning's</u> newspaper, what would it read? Pretend you are a college intern on the local newspaper staff. Write your obituary and be indifferent, realistic, and truthful. Then question: am I satisfied with that? What would you want it to read instead?

OPPORTUNITY:

Write a testimonial to yourself as if you were being honored near the end of your life. What would you want that testimonial to say? What would you want others to say about you and your accomplishments (be creative here)? How many friends would you want to thank? How many faces of those you have helped would be in the audience?

Vacation Plans or "Honey, Why Won't You Stop and Ask For Directions?"

I will treat today as a priceless violin. One may draw harmony from it and another, discord, yet no one will blame the instrument.—Og Mandino

How did you do in the first OPPORTUNITY? (*I call them opportunities rather than problems or exercises. Who wants problems and who wants to exercise?*) Are you satisfied with your obituary? If you are not pleased with your death notice, do not be discouraged. There cannot be too many people alive today who think they have attained every goal by which they would like to be remembered. But remember, the past is the past. And the future lies ahead. How did you do on the second OPPORTUNITY? Were you creative enough to think of new experiences that you would like to have, accomplishments you want to complete, or qualities that you wish to adopt? Later in this book, you will learn how to brainstorm new ideas that remain latent in your subconscious and you will find an endless supply of things you want to achieve in your lifetime.

Next, let's introduce an equation. *Great, another opportunity!* As I mentioned in the preceding paragraph, the past is the past and if we are not satisfied with it, no matter. There is nothing we can do about it—so forget it! For many of us, that is not so easy to do. Our fretting over the past often controls what we do in the future. If we have failed to achieve a particular goal once before, many times we conclude that we will never be successful. But that is not the case. We must learn to unchain and let go of our negative past so it does not become a burden to carry uphill toward the future.

Motivational coach and best-selling author Anthony Robbins has instructed top Olympic athletes, premier business executives, and presidents of countries, including the United States. In his book, *Awaken the Giant Within*, Robbins offers a simple formula relating to this point. It is:

P ≠ F

P stands for "THE PAST." And F represents "THE FUTURE." *The past <u>does not equal</u> the future.*[7] What a concept! I do not think too many of us would have a tough time with that one. Could we deny the truthfulness of this simple equation? Of course, we may cite the old epigram: "Those who do not learn the lessons of history are doomed to repeat them." So, if we go through our lives making mistakes and do not learn from them, then I suppose history can repeat itself. But, the key for those who seek to move forward is to accept that formula. If we are a little cynical, we may want to modify it to say, "The past does not *necessarily* equal the future."

Therefore, if we have been unsuccessful in achieving our goals in the past, it does not necessarily mean we will fail in the future. So, discard the past, as the Beatles sang, "Let it Be." Believe in the future. That is where our lives are.

If we ever have any doubt about setting ambitious goals in our lives, we can listen to children. While driving down the road one day with my kids, my oldest son (a seven year old at the time) said to me, "Dad, I'm going to become a doctor once I finish playing pro football!"

"Oh yeah?" I said, astounded. Boy, this kid has his second career figured out before his eighth birthday, and I had not planned what we were going to eat for dinner that night. "That's great, son," I said. "Why do you want to be a doctor after you finish playing pro football?"

"So I can keep my mansion!" the lad proclaimed.

After I finished laughing, I marveled at the boy's childhood plans. Well, I knew I had to work a bit on his value structure; however, don't all of us wish we had a child's vision? What could we do with an unspoiled, young person's passion kindling under our dreams?

Do we have a plan for our lives? A map of our travels here on this planet? Do we have written objectives with assigned deadlines? Most of us say, "What would we want to do something like that for? Life is for living, not planning! Live for the moment! Have some spontaneity!" Do we want to take the fun out of life by mapping out each moment like it was a fire-escape plan from an office building?

Have you ever planned a vacation? Dumb question, huh? We often allow projects at the office slide for a while, ignore the mess that needs to be cleaned up in the garage, and if we owe Uncle Sam some change, we procrastinate filing our tax return until the evening of April 14. But a vacation? Well, we have that itinerary scouted out to the last nanosecond. We know when we are leaving, when we get to our destination, what we are going to do and see when we get there, how much we have to spend, etc. Why do we have a game plan about a vacation, planning nearly every single moment?

"We only have one week!" we rationalize. "We have to make the most of it. And, besides, it's costing us a bundle! And we won't get another one until next year!"

True, vacations are limited time ventures that often are quite expensive. They do deserve lengthy, meticulous, and careful planning.

But, why don't we plan our lives?

Our lifetime. It costs us everything we have.

Yes, we only have one life, at least here on earth. And guess what folks—it is a vacation for our soul. Psychologist and author Dr. Wayne Dyer cites the ancient proverb, "We are not humans who are having a spiritual experience, but rather, we are spiritual beings having a human experience." Since this is our soul's sole vacation at Club Earth, we should make the most of it. Our life is worth some careful planning. And it means more than retirement accounts or mapping out a financial plan for our children's education, although they are vital things we need to develop a strategy for. We need a plan for our life and its *purpose*. It is worth it. Our life is worthy of substantive goals, loving relationships, and lasting contribution to our families, friends, and communities.

True, often times we face setbacks, challenges, and unfortunate experiences while on vacation. We can get our wallet lifted by a pickpocket, the airline can lose our luggage, and our hotel reservation may be deleted from the computer. In our travels we may find that the taxi driver does not speak English and will take us for a 100-mile tour of

Manhattan instead of down the block. We eat a bad kiwi in Fiji. The kids beat each other senseless in the back seat of the van. We get seasick on the Caribbean cruise or we drop from heat exhaustion in Disney World. But what do our spouses or friends say when these things happen? "Come now, don't let it spoil the whole trip!"

What are goals?

There is nothing, but first, a dream.—Carl Sandburg

In learning "management by objectives," I was taught that goals were something that could never be achieved. Goals were impalpable and only represented the ideal, the direction we should be pointed toward. Objectives, on the other hand, were tangible. For example, we may have a goal to "be healthy." But what is health? How do we measure it? How do we know when we achieve it? We do not get overwhelmed by those questions, but rather, set objectives to help direct us toward the goal. For example:

Goal: Achieve greater health.

Objective No. 1: Get eight hours of sleep a night.

Objective No. 2: Eat balanced, low fat meals.

Objective No. 3: Stop smoking.

Objective No. 4: Engage in aerobic exercise five times a week for at least thirty minutes.

Etc. We could have dozens of objectives to beat the path to our goal. If we take action to achieve those objectives and receive some positive results, we can make the statement with reasonable assuredness, "Yes, I am healthy as I can control."

We may have lots of passions inside of us that we might want to call goals. We may want to win a million dollars in the lottery, be discovered and become a movie star, create a worldwide business, become the great American best-selling novelist, etc. Those types of yearnings are usually unclear aspirations, pipe dreams, or fairy godmother wishes. They are not goals.

But some people do *earn* a million dollars a year, *work* to become famous movie actors, *start* their own successful entrepreneurial venture, and *write* good marketable novels. How do they do it? By dreaming more? By wishing harder? By having more luck? Do they just have more innate talent than the average Josephine? Talent helps, I am sure, but talent alone does not a success make. Usually, these individuals have more than that. First, yes, they do have a dream. It is a dream that possesses them. It is something that they have converted to a specific goal and concentrated on for years. Second, their "goals" have a plan of action that includes specific objectives. They exude high productivity skills. In other words, productivity is anything that forwards us toward our goal. Next, and more important, they set deadlines (or better yet "victory dates") for their accomplishments. Also, they possess determination. Finally, they concentrate their energy behind their ultimate plan and as the sports-equipment manufacturer suggests, they "Just do it!"

Goals start as dreams. Sometimes, life frustrates us to the point that we even refuse to dream. We need to take a lesson from Cinderella, and no matter how dreary our circumstances, the path to the prince's ball starts with a dream. A dream is something that cannot be taken away from us. It is intensely personal. And it can be quite powerful. Most celebrities, sports heroes, famous artists, successful politicians, and affluent entrepreneurs, rarely say when achieving their success, "I never dreamed of this!" Only winners of the lottery say that. More likely, those true triumphant goal-achievers say, "I've been dreaming of this all my life."

Here is one small example. Lanny Frattare was a young boy whose only dream was to become a baseball sportscaster.

"I remember at a very early age, sitting with my tape recorder," Frattare said. "I would practice play-by-play. I wanted to be like my hero—Mel Allen. Growing up in upstate New York, you couldn't help listening to Allen describe the Yankee games."[8]

Frattare never thought of any other career. He focused. He practiced. He persevered. Today, he is living his dream—he does play-by-play baseball broadcasting on radio and television and has called more than 4,000 games as the "Voice of the Pittsburgh Pirates."

Yes, Cinderella, dreams do come true. But first, we must convert them into goals. And that means making critical choices and decisions.

3

The House That Goals Built—Making Choices and Decisions

For a man's house is his castle.—Sir Edward Coke

Have you ever had the fortune, or the curse, of building a new home? Some people have in their mind's eye the perfect home and all its accouterments. They hire an architect and explain all their concepts. Others look and see the home that they desire jump out at them from a magazine page. Others shop for a home endlessly until they walk in the door of their personal palace that contains, all, or at least many, of the visions in their dreams. It does not matter whether we build from scratch, pick a design from a homebuilder, or move into an existing structure. The process is exciting. The anticipation is thrilling. The feeling of moving into any new home is usually glorious—at least until the mortgage payment arrives.

In building a home of our own design, however, there is a process that must be followed in a particular order:

First, we must select the site on a solid foundation on which to construct our house. We take great care in selecting the location because once we start building, we cannot move our home—unless of course, we want to live, as the "Motivational Speaker" character of the late actor Chris Farley of "Saturday Night Live" did, *"in a trailer down by the river!"* The foundation of our life is our purpose. Before we decide what building to create, we must select the proper foundation on which to build it. Before we conclude what goals we are going to pursue, we have to determine what is the purpose of our life. In the movie *Star Wars*, Luke Skywalker knew his mission was to save the princess to lead the rebellion against Darth Vadar and the evil Empire. All of his actions were geared toward that purpose. His interstellar companion, Han Solo, wandered around the galaxy getting into trouble with no particular aim other than to elude bounty hunters until, like Luke, he found a worthy purpose to pursue.

Second, like the three little pigs, we have to select the material of which we want to build our house. Should it be constructed of straw, sticks, or bricks? Unless we plan to get visited by a big bad wolf anytime soon, our selection of framing material for construction is up to us. As long as it can withstand the huffs and puffs of the weather of life and keep us safe and warm at night, it is our choice.

Third, no matter what design of home we would like to build, we need a blueprint. That design for action is necessary before we attempt to insert Tab A into Slot B or our house will be a disaster. Our blueprint—our design for action—is our goal-and-objective strategy for achieving our purpose.

Finally, unless we are trained as a master carpenter, we better get some help from the experts. We can build our own abode, but it will take training, practice, and attention to the proper building skills. Sure, we will make mistakes. We will put a window in backwards, not allow enough room for the bathroom door to open, or accidentally glue the toilet seat up, but if we follow the instructions and persist, we will eventually finish it! In our life, we will attract constant teachers as well, instructing the proper way to improve our effectiveness. Parents, friends, families, and spouses can be helpful instructors with proper lessons for good living. We will never be perfect, but the pursuit of a worthy life is an enjoyable quest. In this book, our building skills are called the ABC strategies of success. But to begin, let's go back to the foundation.

Why Goals?

In the long run, we only hit the target we aim at.—Henry David Thoreau

There are plenty of goal-oriented self-improvement books on the market. There are even books for sale that tell us how to live *without* goals. There are many publications appropriate to assist busy men and women juggling a career and family. There are volumes suitable for hyper Type-A achievers, and still others apropos for laid-back Type-B personalities. There are hundreds, if not thousands, of sources to help guide us through a productive, meaningful, and satisfying life no matter what cards we were dealt.

With all of this educational information, expert teachers, proper role models, and encouraging coaches everywhere on the planet, how come more people do not move toward their virtually unlimited potential? Is it because the die is cast before individuals can mold themselves? Is it only the rich who have inherited wealth who achieve financial success? Can only the insensitive, wicked, and dishonest people climb their way up the corporate ladder? Is it only the lucky or deceptive who succeed in love?

I believe in the old adage: "You can lead a horse to water, but you cannot make him drink." The decision to drink from life's opportunity is available to practically every individual that lives in the free nations of our planet. And that determination depends on how thirsty we are. Are life's winners just lucky? Researcher Thomas Stanley, author of *The Millionaire Next Door* and *The Millionaire Mind*, says most highly successful people are self-made and have reached their pinnacle of success by choosing a vocation that they love. Stanley says among the top success factors these people have are:

- *Integrity*—being honest with themselves and others;
- *Discipline*—applying effort;
- *Social Skills*—getting along with others;
- a *Supportive Spouse*; and
- *Hard Work*—i.e., working more than most people.[9]

These individuals have goals. Goals provide the energy, the juice of life. For example, psychologists say that striving toward a long-term life goal is an essential feature of the human sense of self.[10] I believe that most people who do not achieve what they define as happiness or success do not lack the ability. They simply do not have exhilarating goals that excite them! They never sit down to think about what they want to accomplish. All they have is weak, blurry wishes with unclear motives. They want to be more successful, but have not defined what they believe success is. Our goals must be exciting, real, and definite. It matters less what goal we have. It matters more how inspired and energized we are in working toward it.

What will life without goals provide us? Paraphrasing the Cheshire Cat in *Alice In Wonderland*, "If you don't know where you are going, then any road will take you there." But those who chart their course and monitor their progress usually end up at their own desired destination.

In this section, we discussed why goals are necessary to achieve what we define as success. However, it is the pursuit of these worthy objectives that can give us more pleasure than the actual achievement of them. Our fuzzy dream of a better world for others and ourselves can be translated into a clear goal by simply defining what it is we want, and assigning a "victory date" for its accomplishment. A strong belief that our dreams can become reality is essential to effective goal-setting. In fact, this belief is the first step in achieving them.

The only thing certain about five years from now is that we will be five years older. Everything else is up to us. What road we will take or even choose not to take will dictate where we will be. That is why the path of our lives is dictated by our choices.

Choices

Two roads diverged in a wood, and I—
I took the one less traveled by,
And that has made all the difference.—Robert Frost

There is a story about a very religious art aficionado who sought the answer to an enigma. This man was very fond of Mary, the Blessed Mother of Jesus, but he found it troubling that in all the famous paintings of the Holy Mother cradling the infant Jesus, she was never brightly smiling. Instead she only appeared to be quietly content. Distressed about this quandary, he sought an answer from the local parish priest. The priest was equally perplexed and suggested the gentleman seek advice from the local bishop. After making an appointment with the bishop, the inquisitive man posed the same question. Stumped for an answer, the bishop recommended that the man seek an audience with the Pope in Rome. After numerous attempts over many years, the man finally received an audience with the Holy Father. When asked about the mystery about the less-than-beaming Mary, the Pope responded that there were some questions that could not be answered on earth. Frustrated, the religious art lover returned home. Several years later, the man passed away and his spirit traveled to heaven. At the Pearly Gates, he met St. Peter. When St. Peter asked the newly arrived soul if he had any questions about heaven, the man again asked his mortal query about the paintings of the Blessed Mother. "Well," St. Peter responded, "Why don't you go right in and ask her yourself." After this long fruitless search through all the holy men, the man found

Mary and asked her, "In all the famous earthly paintings of you cradling the infant Jesus, you never appear to be joyously smiling—why?"

Mary looked down and said softly, "Well, I was kind of hoping for a girl."

Perhaps there are some things in life we cannot choose. But, with the exception of our sex and who our parents and siblings are, our life is full of options we can select.

Here is another equation to ponder:

$$L = \Sigma C$$

L represents LIFE, our life. The symbol Σ stands for "the sum of." And C equals CHOICES, the choices we make in our life. In written terms:

Our life is equal to the sum of all of the choices we make.

While this formula may not apply to babies and young children, it very much is pertinent to adults. Our life up to this point is the result of a series of choices and decisions we have made when we confronted the problems and opportunities before us. The reason you are reading this book right now is because you have chosen to. *We* made the decision to work for our current employer in a chosen profession, not some Greek god in the sky throwing thunderbolts down to earth. If we are married, our selection of a mate was entirely our judgment. Our financial condition is, in the end, our responsibility. The food we eat, our mental outlook, and the physical activity we partake in largely determine our general health (excluding heredity and sudden illnesses). As adults, our degree of knowledge and intellect is impacted more by our own choices than by whether our parents were rich or poor or the quality of the primary or secondary school system we attended. In other words, if we do not like where we are in life, there a few, if any, excuses.

I know these are strong assertions that many could counter with sociological, psychological, and cultural arguments. Many will rush to point out the myriad of studies that cite people who have been severely and negatively impacted by their upbringing, abusive parents, inadequate schooling, depraved finances, etc., and therefore have fewer opportunities. But unless there is a medical or mental illness that results in incapacitation, I believe all of these excuses are simply that, excuses. What the studies do not explain is how numerous individuals, facing the worst of circumstances, created remarkable achievements for themselves, and worked their way up through the bottom ranks of society to become leaders in education, business, government, religion, art, and in every facet of life. For every conglomeration of adults stuck in the mire of poverty, there are a select few entrepreneurs who began their business by selling articles out of their basement, on the street, or out of the trunk of their car, eventually achieving affluence.

Paul Snyder was a college dropout. Raised in working-class Buffalo, New York, he wanted to own his own business. One day he got an idea. At that time, many local grocery stores sold ground beef, but few sold hamburgers in patties. Paul bought a hamburger patty maker and purchased large amounts of ground beef. He pressed the meat into patties, froze them, and then went to market to market, selling ground beef patties to stores out of the trunk of his car. That was the start of what became a huge frozen-food business. Paul later pursued numerous other entrepreneurial ventures. He eventually developed a hotel in downtown Buffalo, one of the cornerstones of the industrial city's downtown Renaissance in the 1980s, and many other business ventures.

"I get so many ideas every morning," Paul once told me while I was interviewing him for a local radio news station. "The only frustrating thing is that I can only pursue one or two a day."

Paul is a man who created something out of nothing. He did not need a college degree, rich parents, or a government handout to get started. He took matters into his own hands, took his idea, and ran with it. The great Baroque composer Johann Sebastian Bach said something similar. He did not have trouble thinking of melodies. Rather, he just tried to avoid tripping over them when he got up in the morning. The *International Journal of Entrepreneurship and Innovation* reported in 2002 that goal-setting is vital in nurturing potential entrepreneurs and suggests that business schools should influence individuals' "self-belief," which is a prerequisite for achieving future entrepreneurial goals.[11]

Despite being abused physically and emotionally in childhood, there are the numerous examples of people that have climbed out of despair to become shining role models. Take one of the most widely admired and richest women in America—Oprah Winfrey. Abuse and a lack of self-esteem consumed her youth. Today she is a role model for millions of Americans. In her book *Making the Connection* written with Bob Greene, Winfrey described her successful battle with weight problems by deciding what was right for her: "The most important part is to understand that it's not as much about the weight as it is about making the connection. That means looking after yourself every day and putting forth your best effort to love yourself enough to do what's best for you."[12] The woman who late-night comedians poked fun at for her ups and downs in weight took control of her life. Do you think you could run a twenty-six mile marathon? Oprah did.

In spite of many that are raised in disadvantaged single-parent homes in the squalor of the inner city or the rural mountains, there is the cream of the crop that rise to the pinnacle of their potential. Look at many of our nation's presidents: Bill Clinton was raised in an indigent household by his mother in rural Arkansas; Ronald Reagan struggled to make a living on his own through the depression years; Jimmy Carter was raised on humble farm in Georgia; Richard Nixon grew up in a plain Quaker household; and Lyndon Johnson grew up poor in rugged, rural Texas. And does anyone remember Abraham Lincoln? You know, the guy who was born in a log cabin in Kentucky and raised in a meager household in Illinois?

Oh, but you say those are the exceptions! Exceptions? Yes, the folks who are superior in intellect, in personal ambition, or in chutzpah. They are the freaks of society who become successful despite the odds. Are these cases freaks? Or are they individuals who made many choices in their lives, some bad, but more of them good? We can believe that our destiny is shaped by the art of "fate," or we can believe that our future is molded by us, the artist. I submit to you, the latter is the better alternative.

Our choices and our decisions are what shape our destiny. We need to make quality decisions if we want our life to be carved into the shape that we desire in our minds.

The First Step—Decisions

When you get to a fork in the road, take it.—Yogi Berra

Every December 31st, especially if celebrating the coming New Year at a party, we all proclaim our New Year's resolutions. Everybody does one time or another. Even my son once vowed to make his bed every day in the New Year. And surprisingly, it lasted a week and a half—much longer than Dad predicted! Have you ever failed to live up to your resolutions? Well, that's a stupid question, isn't it? Do you know why New Year's resolutions rarely last to Ground Hog's Day? It is *not* because we are failures. It is *not* because we do not want to see a change in our behavior. It is *not* because we lack "willpower." *It is because* we have made powerless decisions about our goals.

The word decision is derived from the Latin *decidere*—de (off) and caedere (to cut) or in other words, to "cut off from."[13] That means when we make a decision, we are cutting ourselves off from any other possible outcome. When Dorothy met the Scarecrow in the *Wizard of Oz*, she faced a fork in the road. She sought an opinion of which way to go, but the Scarecrow could not decide which direction was the better alternative. He claimed it was because he did not have a brain. However, she had a choice to either go left or right or return back to Munchkinland. She eventually chose a path, relying on her intuition. If, by chance, Dorothy chose to remain at the fork because she could not decide, that, in itself, is a decision. "Indecisiveness" is a decision to do nothing. We often decide to remain stagnant because we fear making the wrong choice. But at all times, it was Dorothy's option and so it also is ours.

Some people do make permanent changes to their lives by making firm decisions about how they are going to live. It is the first step in the right direction. They are the ones described with the moral fiber, iron will, perseverance, and stick-to-it-tiveness to doggedly remain focused on their goals and achieve their definition of success. Are these special tenacious people given blessed diligent qualities from the god of resolution? Or are they only people who have made a clean-cut decision? They are ready to, as Shakespeare said, "wear this world out to the ending doom" and are unwilling to accept any other alternative than their stated goal. They are decision-makers. And so are we.

We can decide to stay with our current employer or to look for another job. We have chosen to enter our personal relationships. As stated before, we did not choose our parents, but we *do* have the option of selecting our attitude toward them. Now, you have decided to read this book as I decided to write it. Hopefully, you have decided to finish it, take advantage of the opportunities in it by writing down your ideas, and take positive action. Some will decide to read, but not to finish. Others will decide to finish, but not write down their ideas. A select few will finish, apply the concepts, and see clear, positive, and definite changes in their daily life. In any case, at all times it is our decision.

When we make staunch decisions, we give them commitment to back them up. But sometimes commitment is not enough. We must have, as management expert Ken Blanchard, author of the business mega-seller of the 1980s, *The One Minute Manager*, says, "commitment to our commitment."[14] Our pledge of commitment is a covenant in which our integrity is based. If we vow to start an exercise program, stop eating fatty foods, or begin working on the Great American novel, our willpower alone will not get us all the way. Willpower is just the man behind the curtain and not the great and powerful OZ. As the traveling quartet found out at the Wizard's palace, our demanding commitment to our integrity—not some magical sorcerer—will get us brains, a heart, a home, and the nerve.

We must make a true decision. One that is clear, understandable, and supported by enough good reasons to propel us toward our objective. That does not mean that the exact path to our Emerald-City goal is laid out in yellow bricks. In fact, there may not be an obvious navigable road at all. We may have to cut our own path, often become sidetracked, make mistakes, and we may be required to change our route. But the ultimate destination is what we have defined as our "OZ." When we really decide, we are the Wizards, and we are already on our way. That is, Dorothy, once we understand how to click our heels three times.

Sometimes decisions are made with no clear-cut trail. Calverinian leader Hannibal led his troops toward the Italian Alps two centuries before the birth of Christ. There was no path across the mountain range, and his forces had no idea how to cross to get to the ultimate destination. Hannibal said, "We will find a way or we will make one." Now, ladies and gentleman, that's a decision. Are you ready to make such powerful decisions?

OPPORTUNITY:

Write down three major decisions that you have been putting off. Don't worry about making the wrong choice just yet. Just write "as if" you have decided.

1.

2.

3.

In this chapter, we have discussed how choices dictate our lives. We do not mean the choices that are made by others for us, but the choices we make for ourselves. But we cannot make choices blindly. Even though we cannot see our passageway to our goal, we must know why we want to get there in the first place. Before we cast our decisions into unyielding cement, we must first identify the noble purpose of our lives. In other words, a solid foundation must lie below our dreams.

4

A Solid Foundation—Developing a Personal Purpose for a Sense of Destiny

The house fell not: for it was founded upon a rock.—Matthew 6:34

Before construction begins on our house of goals, we must decide *where* to build it. Should it be on the seashore? That would be beautiful, especially if we can afford the land. Then again, there are severe storms or hurricanes that can damage it. Should our house lay safe in a secluded forest affording us peace and tranquillity? That would be charming, if we enjoy living that far away from others. Then again, if we have special needs, we may need to be closer to civilization.

Where should we build our house? There is no uniform answer for everyone. It is a matter of personal preference. Whether it is by the water or in the busy city, whatever feels right to us is the correct solution. However, no matter where we chose to place our home, it must be constructed on solid ground. Would we erect our dream home on a sinkhole? I think not. Would we construct the foundation of our lives on a loose, sandy surface, subject to erosion from severe weather? Most builders would advise against it. Would we establish our lifetime dream dwelling precariously balanced on the side of a mountain that is known for mud, rock, or snow slides? That would be pretty risky. Without a firm foundation on which to set our home—our lifetime goals—it can wiped away with a single blow of nature's breath. Our goals must evolve from a stable base, impervious from uncontrollable ferocious forces—the unexpected harsh elements that erupt in our lives. This solid foundation is our purpose, our principles, and our fundamental way of living.

Goals do not a lifetime make, nor are they our sole intent for living. We need a profound purpose for our lives. We need to live a life that is based on a worthwhile tenet. You have probably heard of the riddle that states: "I am at a place that no matter what direction I step, I am going north, where am I?" The answer is, of course, "The South Pole."

Our lives should be no different. No matter what goal we have in mind, we must have a certain code of conduct—a set of principles and purpose on which we live. Our principles should not vacillate in the wind of everyday pressures. We do not need to pursue our goals at all costs, sacrificing any ideal or behavior to get us there. In Jules Verne's classic novel *Around the World in Eighty Days*, nothing could dissuade the proper Englishman Phinneas Fogg from his goal of traveling the earth in four-score days. He would travel by rail, steamer, or elephant to reach his goal, no matter what the monetary cost. But when traveling through India, Fogg crossed the path of a woman who was going to be sacrificed against her will in a barbaric native ritual. Saving the woman meant setting Fogg off track and threatening to ruin achievement of his quest. However, when faced with pursuing his immediate goal or doing what his principles instructed him, there was no question of what he would do. He rescued the woman before proceeding on his journey. Did he make his goal anyway? In case you do not know, I will not tell you here. Read the novel. It is a wonderful example of goal-setting.

What does this mean for us? We not only need the right goals that give our life enjoyment, we also need to endeavor toward them guided by righteous principles.

Management and leadership consultant Dr. Stephen Covey is noted for popularizing awareness of a "mission statement" that is based on

"True North" principles for both individuals and organizations.[15] Covey states that our principles should work as a moral compass, always directing us toward our true purpose. To discover our principles, Covey says, we must listen to our own conscience. That is a difficult chore, but one that is necessary. It may be more arduous than pursuing our toughest goals. But once we are at peace with our principles that become our code of living, the quest for our goals becomes much easier.[16] Developing principles makes us responsibly proactive rather than reactive to events that occur in our lives. We know that our actions are not dictated by the conduct of others. And we also discover that our ability to act reaches out beyond our immediate grasp.

If you have ever walked by your local YMCA, you have seen the triangle logo, representing "Body, Mind, and Spirit." Like legs on a three-legged stool, these three entities must be in good shape for a balanced, healthy life to remain standing. Take away one leg and the stool is sure to tumble. Other experts often mention a fourth entity necessary for a well-balanced individual: nourishing relationships. Our social lives also need to be cultivated for us to be truly happy people.

Psychologist Abraham Maslow's "hierarchy of needs" theorized how human needs evolve from basic physical survival to a point of self-actualization. According to Maslow, self-actualizing people who have "come to a high level of maturation, health, and self-fulfillment, have so much to teach us that sometimes they seem almost like a different breed of human beings."[17] Other experts have modified Maslow's pioneering work. Covey states that each human being has four basic needs: "To Live, To Love, To Learn, and to Leave a Legacy."[18] These four needs reflect the entities we are talking about:

- **To Live** (Physical) our health and well-being;
- **To Love** (Social) the quality of our relationships;
- **To Learn** (Mental) the need for growth in our lives; and
- **To Leave a Legacy** (Spiritual) our contribution to others.

First, our physical needs are obvious. We need air, water, and food to survive. To maintain our healthy life, we need to take care of our physical bodies with exercise, proper diet, sufficient rest, and safe living practices. But no human being is usually satisfied with only having only a soundness of body. There must be more.

Second, we need to love, for that is a special emotion that separates us from the rest of the animal kingdom. However, many scientific studies show that even animals will wither and die if they only receive physical needs of food, water, and shelter, but are denied the closeness or affinity with other animals of their kind. What makes us humans any different? We need to develop quality relationships within our family, close connections within our circle of friends, and for most of us, a devotional relationship with a Supreme Being. Those who lack these critical relationships, or feel they are denied this "love," can simply create it by loving others. The purpose of life, said founding father Benjamin Franklin, is to "love and be loved." Notice that our love must be given first before it is returned. This is no accident of syntax. Our *expression* of love for others, not dependency on what others provide us, must come first to be effective. This "love giving" is a critical need.

Third, continual mental improvement and growth is also necessary for us who want to discover our true potential. Development of our mental capacities has progressed since Neanderthals drew pictures on cave walls. We came out of the cave first to walk upright and eventually to walk the moon. Each of us desires to grow mentally, develop our careers, hone our skills, and discover the mysteries of our world. There are very few people who are content at their current level of understanding. They want to reach new levels of awareness in their daily life. We, as human beings, are not granted the instinctive powers of the animal kingdom. We must improve our skills, not only to grow, but also to survive.

Finally, as we grow older and recognize there will be a conclusion of our mission on Starship Earth, most of us ponder what our lives are all about. As mentioned before, few on their deathbed are thinking about what their bank balance is, or if the honors in their trophy case are polished. We think about what our lives meant to others, our families, our communities, our society, and our God. Though every individual builds strength by personal responsibility and strives to be self-sufficient, we have an innate need to belong to something greater than ourselves. The talented musician desires to play in an orchestra. The well-trained athlete wants to make the Olympic team. The successful corporate manager wants to contribute to the satisfaction of the customers of his or her company. The newlywed wants to be involved in a loving marriage and raise an affectionate family. No man or woman is an island. We want to make a difference with our lives. We want to serve our God on this mission. We long to leave a legacy that sets a loving example for our children and the world to follow.

In author Faith Popcorn's book *Clicking*, which depicts future trends in the United States, she reveals that more and more people are looking for spiritual guidance and direction, though not everyone cites it as God. "We're at the start of a Great Awakening," Popcorn writes. "A time of spiritual upheaval and religious revival. A time to dig into the core principles of the past to provide some sort of anchoring for the unknown ahead. What's different about this awakening is that there's very little agreement on who or what God is, what constitutes worship, and what the ritualistic outpouring means for the future direction of our civilization." After the so-called "me-decade" of the 1980s and the stock market rise and spending spree in the 1990s, we now are searching for our roots and values. As Popcorn writes, "We're looking for the essence of ourselves—our lost souls."[19] In addition, after the terrorist attacks on the United States on September 11, 2001, many surveys show that Americans have become more spiritual.

We have all seen people whose behaviors within these four categories are out of balance. There are the athletes who may be consumed by their physical condition and health, at the cost of sacrificing their relationships. Loving parents may spend their daily life nourishing their children, but neglect their own physical and mental growth. There is the scholar or businessperson that works to the point of frenzy but returns home with a withered body, a depressed spirit, and a malnourished marriage. And there are the generous givers who play a pious portrayal to the point of martyrdom by constantly giving to others, but rarely taking on the support they need to sustain their own life and happiness.

Our principles are more than values. And they are uniquely ours. God granted human beings several qualities that the rest of the earthly creatures do not share. According to Covey, they are self-awareness, a conscience, independent will, and creative imagination.[20] We are aware of our presence on this planet with God-given gifts, and we know in our heart that we are here for a reason. Like Jiminy Cricket counseling the naive wooden puppet Pinocchio, our conscience is always around to guide us to the right path. But we do have to listen to it, trust it, and believe that our instincts are the right ones. As human beings, our independent will cannot be controlled by anyone other than ourselves. Others can imprison us and hold our bodies bound, but only we can incarcerate our mind. In most cases, we have the power to choose. Finally, unlike animals, human beings do not rely on instinct alone in making choices. Our imagination and thoughts are limitless. It can guide us to, as Captain Kirk of *Star Trek* fame would say, "go where no [one] has gone before." Or back on earth, as Albert Einstein said, "Imagination is everything." These characteristics separate us from the remainder of the animal kingdom and call to us a greater purpose.

So what is our purpose? The age-old query, now a hackneyed question, is: "What is the purpose of life?" Dr. Leo Buscaglia, the world-renown University of Southern California professor who created a college course on "Love" and authored several books on the subject, told a story in his lectures about the quest for the "meaning of life." A man searching for the answer to this elusive question is told that a sagacious guru on top of the highest mountain had the solution. After a tortuous and perilous ascent up the rocky peak, the questioner finds the guru and asks, "What's the meaning of life?"

The guru responds simply, "Life is a bowl of cherries."

"What?" the seeker exclaimed. "Life is a bowl of cherries? That is the stupidest thing I have ever heard in my life. What kind of idiot would believe that life is a bowl of cherries?"

The guru asked nervously, "You mean it isn't?"

The big secret about the meaning of "life" is: we do not need to know. We only need to know the meaning of *our own* life. As the saying goes, "the purpose of life is a life with purpose." Again, our choices come into play. What is the meaning of *our* life?

One way to discover our purpose is to write a personal mission statement. There are several excellent books on the subject, so I urge you to seek those guides. We must reach down to our own souls to discover our "purpose." Our purpose is not our goals. It is a set of guiding standards that shepherd us as we travel along the right course.

Purpose statements, according to author Laurie Beth Jones in *The Path*, have three qualities:

- They should be only a single sentence;

- They should be clear enough to be understood by a twelve-year-old; and

- They should be simple enough to be recited by memory at gun-point.[21]

Jones provides an excellent guide on forming a mission statement by determining what a mission statement is not, discovering our deep inner interests, choosing active verbs that give a mission passion, and wrapping our mission in all parts of our life. Our mission is not just our job. It is not only our personal life. All parts of our life must be congruous to be effective. Mahatma Ghandi said, "A person cannot do good in one role of life and do ill in another." The Bible tells us that we are all one body. Jesus said to his followers, "If your right hand sins, cut it off. Better to enter the kingdom of heaven crippled than to damn your entire soul." The message makes the point that our principles apply twenty-four hours a day in all roles in our life. We do not shed our souls when we go to the office on Monday morning. Nor should we pack away our ambition when we leave for the weekend. Our principles never take the day off and cannot be corrupted by external forces or internal fears.

Mission or purpose statements are becoming more common in today's non-profit agencies as well as for-profit corporations. If these declarations are good enough for multi-billion dollar organizations, they should be good enough for us as individuals. But take your time. Mission statements should be developed after much contemplation and can be amended.

Purpose statements will save us time and tribulations. No longer will we have to debate whether a particular action is worthy of our attention, concern, or involvement. If it corresponds to our planned and heartfelt purpose, it deserves our action. If it does not, then we know not to waste our time with it. Once writing a mission or purpose statement, we will discover the difference between the leaders in life and those who only suffer through it. Be a leader. Let's form a purpose statement that is uniquely ours, a mission that reflects our inner soul, and motivates us to fulfill our destiny.

OPPORTUNITY:

Take the time to write your own personal purpose statement. It may help to obtain one of the many books or articles on the subject of writing a mission statement. Write it down, keep it simple, make it active, commit it to memory, and think of it every day.

Back to our house of goals. As mentioned before, when we think about whether we want a two-story colonial, or a split-level ranch, we must first select solid ground on which to build. Prior to considering whether we prefer a Jacuzzi in the bathroom or a bay window overlooking a resplendent flower garden, we must decide which way our house will face. In advance of choosing a stone wood-burning hearth or a modern natural-gas fireplace, we must be certain that our home is not built on a sinkhole. In other words, a solid foundation will hold up to all the major obstacles and changes we will face in life. Next, how will we decide our preferences of what to construct our home from—straw, sticks, or bricks?

5

Framing Our Home—Our Values and Beliefs

Decisions are easy when values are clear.—Roy Disney, brother of Walt Disney

The story of the three little pigs is a storybook analogy of building our home of goals. After laying a solid foundation on which to build, our choice of building materials is indeed our next critical step. But the issue of what we build our house with is more important than just avoiding constructing our dream home out of straw or sticks. Our choice is a little different than the trio of swine rushing to erect their first abode.

For example, what harm would there be for Oinker Uno to construct a thatch house if there were no other materials available? Would a big, bad wolf huff and puff, and blow it down? Thatch homes fabricated out of straw are not unusual in many parts of the world. Sometimes, that is the only building material available in many locales. If a typhoon wipes them out on a South Pacific island, they can be quickly replaced when the sun comes out again.

For Neanderthals, a cave was an appropriate shelter to accomplish their basic mission of staying warm and safe by building a fire and eluding the saber-toothed tiger. For the Plains Native Americans, teepees were the chosen domicile due to their nomadic lifestyle. For leaders in wartime, a steel-reinforced concrete bunker might be appropriate quarters.

The point is, whatever we favor for our construction materials is entirely up to us. However, if we are building in the far north with bitter winter winds, I doubt whether we would select straw and mud to line our walls. If we live in an area with high populations of termites, I question if we would elect to erect a home of sticks like the second little porker. And if we had a big, bad wolf threatening to breathe down our necks, we might take a little more time and build a house of bricks similar to hog number three. Everything depends on your individual situation. Completing the metaphor, instead of choosing straw, sticks, or bricks, we must select our values that frame our home.

The Nails—Our Values

Always do right. This will gratify some people, and astonish the rest.
—Mark Twain

Values are conceptions—often culturally influenced and personally motivating—of desirable ways of behaving such as living healthily, respecting tradition, and possessing ambition. They can also be desirable end-states such as equality or friendship.[22] And our values, whether we are conscious of them or not, drive our behavior. There are basically two kinds of values that motivate people: *Positive* and *Negative*, guided on the noted pleasure-pain principle. Positive values are those that we try to pursue to give us pleasure. Succeeding in living up to our values "fulfills a particular, highly abstract goal."[23] Thus, positive values can guide our behavior toward our goals. Conversely, negative values, which often cause pain, are those we attempt to avoid. However, we are often confused about our values. Sometimes, we are not certain of what we desire, but we are positive about what we do not want. At least that is what our old romantic partners tell us when they write a

Dear John/Jane letter. And not surprisingly, that is exactly what we tell them when we are the ones with the poison pens.

We should, however, take time to discover what our values are and how important each one is to us. When we do this type of exercise, we discover than many times we have *conflicting* values. That is common. Understanding what motivates us, however, can provide us with a force for achieving our goals easier.

What is a positive value? It is something that we find worthy, important, or desirable. We may value wealth. Many people do. We may value a loving relationship. Again, most human beings desire that as well. But we may be surprised upon even a cursory self-examination of our inner thoughts, that values that we may never have put a finger on rise to the surface.

Examples of positive values may be:

- Independence
- Security
- Reputation
- Intimacy
- Integrity
- Health
- Wealth

Examples of negative values may be:

- Frustration
- Loneliness
- Failure
- Humiliation
- Guilt

Again, like our choice of building materials, there is no correct listing of positive values to motivate us forward, nor is there an appropriate combination of negative values we may attempt to avoid. Like snowflakes, the cluster of values among people may appear roughly identical at first glance. But when we look closely at each individual, his or her value design may be radically different. Our choice of values is entirely within us. They will probably change or evolve as we age and face new experiences. You may have no idea what you truly value until you take part in the upcoming OPPORTUNITY.

Also, values are not cut and dried, with our positive values representing the polar opposite of our negative values. We may experience contradictory positive values. For example, we may value "independence" high on our list of positive values. We may desire freedom in our job to do things our way or pursue a career of self-employment. We may not want to rely on others for emotional support and shun close relationships. Right on par with that noble value, we may have also listed "security." We may crave independence and emotional security at the same time. These diametric values may be common in many of us. Though it is certainly acceptable to have conflicting positive values, unless we recognize them, they can be self-sabotaging and keep us from pursuing our goals.

If we ever had a goal we have had trouble reaching, it may be because we had a value conflict. For example, if we desire a close emotional alliance with another person, but at the same time crave independence, the end result may be a series of self-sabotaged relationships. By recognizing this, we can work to resolve our conflicts and get what we want out of life. Recognizing any conflicting values is the first step in making our value structure work for us. How we resolve these potential conflicts is important to our success in achieving our coveted ultimate objectives.

Having a proper understanding of our current values, and how they change over time, is essential for constructing the goals worth striving for in our lives. We need to know not only what our values are, but also how important each individual value is to us. We would not want to spend our life pursuing goals based on low-priority values while ignoring those we truly treasure most. We can brainstorm a list of both positive and negative values and write them down, but often it is a painstaking process deciding how to rank them in importance. Author and business management expert Dr. Ken Blanchard suggests a simple, understandable process for breaking down our values. In his publication *Living Great,* he offers a play-off competition analogy to determine our values. Blanchard uses the metaphor of the college basketball tournament held each March to our values-breakdown comparison. The NCAA first picks sixty-four teams to compete in a sudden-death elimination round. After two rounds, the teams are narrowed down to the "Sweet Sixteen." The following round ends up with the "Elite Eight" and of course, the much ballyhooed "Final Four." Finally, the two remaining winning teams play for the national championship. Blanchard suggests we do the same with our values to determine what is most important to us.

OPPORTUNITY:

Brainstorm your most important sixteen positive values in your life. Then match each value with another one and come to a decision which values are most important to you. Do this a few times until you get to your "Final Four." Do the same with your negative values. That will give you an idea of what is most important to you.

Positive values:

1.

2.

3.

4.

5.

6.

7.

8.

9.

10.

11.

12.

13.

14.

15.

16.

Negative values:

1.

2.

3.

4.

5.

6.

7.

8.

9.

10.

11.

12.

13.

14.

15.

16.

Values drive goals by giving them momentum. They are like the gravitational force of the earth, which can be utilized to propel a spacecraft out of orbit and toward the moon, another planet, or a distant star. We cannot get enough speed to reach our destination in a reasonable amount of time unless we gain enough momentum. Moving toward our positive values and pushing away from our negative values will launch us toward our goal.

Here is an example how values help catapult us toward our goals. In my list of values, I determined that excellent health was in the top-five values. I also listed close personal relationships and fun as priority values in my top sixteen. Many on my list of negative values mirrored the exact opposite of some of my positive values. I obviously did not value sickness and death, nor did I merit loneliness and boredom. Out of these positive and negative values I formed a desired goal: to begin and maintain an exercise and diet regimen that would keep me healthy, and hopefully, alive! My positive values would drive me in the direction of my goal and my negative values would also motivate me away from the opposite.

As you probably know, crash diets do not work for numerous physical and psychological reasons. One main explanation for failed diets is that we are denying ourselves desirable needs and wants—such as carbs! Dieting is painful, and often times works against our own passionate values. Any basic course in psychology will teach us about the opposing forces of pain and pleasure. Pain and pleasure either propel us forward or pull us backward in every action that we make. Comedian George Carlin on his comedy recording *Class Clown* described pain and pleasure growing up attending religious school: "The nuns were always pushing for pain and the kids were always pulling for pleasure!" But kidding aside, pain and pleasure do influence most of our actions. Diets and exercise, for many people, represent pain, and our minds will do just about anything to avoid it. However, if our minds can be convinced that there is a greater pleasure to be obtained by accomplishing a goal and fulfilling our purpose, we will transcend beyond the barrier of pain.

But how? If the supernatural forces of pain and pleasure rule us, how can we break through? We are not just creatures who crave comfort or resist suffering. For example, those that prevailed through unimaginable human suffering in the Nazi death camps had both minds and spiritual purpose that could not be controlled like animals. Viktor Frankl was a Jewish psychologist living in Germany during the Second World War. He is also a survivor of the Nazi concentration camp at Auschwitz. Frankl concluded that those people who survived the apparently hopeless imprisonment and torture did so because they were able to focus on a future not apparent in their current physical experience. Likewise, our life's purpose, illustrated by worthy goals, can break the barrier of pain that prevents our liberation. However, we can use the forces of pain and pleasure for our own motivation, as long as we have a clear goal in mind. Some researchers suggest that we can use both pain and pleasure in pursuing our goal by beginning our journey by framing a goal for its positive opportunities, but once the activity is adopted, reframing in terms of avoiding obstacles may more effectively motivate our actions.[24]

How did I accomplish a consistent successful health program as a goal? *First*, being single at the time, I aspired to improve my physical appearance to appear more attractive to the opposite sex. That's a powerful positive motivator! The *value* of a close personal relationship, therefore, was a positive-motivating factor. *Second*, I wished to rejuvenate my activity in certain sports that I enjoyed when I was younger—another positive promoter of my goal activity. The *value* of "fun" played a role, because in order to enjoy these sports, my body needed to be in a much improved physical condition. *Third*, my father died at a relatively young age, partially due to his poor physical health, obesity, and a sedentary lifestyle. I certainly did not want this to happen to me at such a young age because I valued "life," not "death." This is a continual "negative" obstacle I want to avoid and it always keeps me on the treadmill rather than on the couch. The combination of going-toward-positive values and repelling-from-negative values keep my motivation level high enough to battle the forces that often defeat such goals, (i.e., pain, boredom, and temptation). Although values alone cannot accomplish goals, they are seeds of success that need watering and nurturing from an attentive gardener.

We can learn to use our own value structure to serve as nails to hold together our desired state. Our values can even help identify goals that may be foggy in our mind, and eventually keep us on track as we travel toward our destination. Then, we can be like the *Little Engine That Could*. Despite the odds, the effort, and the pain, we can reach the top of the hill by repeating, "I think I can, I think I can, I think I can." That brings us to another essential ingredient in the recipe for a successful strong house of goals. That is, positive belief.

The 2 X 4's—Our Positive Beliefs

Believe it and you will see it.—*Wayne Dyer*

"Whether you believe you can, or believe you can't, you're right." That quote did not come from a children's book about a little train engine, but it could have. That statement is often attributed to Henry Ford, who changed how the world moved by the belief that he could build automobiles rapidly and inexpensively through an assembly line. As a result, many ordinary people could afford a basic car. But it was no accident of nature. It formed by the belief that something great could evolve out the seeds of ingenuity.

From Proverbs 23:7, the Bible tells us, "As he thinketh in his heart, so is he." Or as leading motivational experts claim: "What the mind can conceive and believe, it can achieve." Now we know how Henry Ford planted his belief.

From the early chapters of the Torah and the later books of the New Testament, to the minds of Greek philosophers and the quiet inner wisdom of Far East masters, one concept is universal: The secret to success is, "as you think, so shall you become." Our thoughts and concepts about our capabilities manifest in our action. Today, computer experts instruct us that the results produced by these marvels of technology can be gummed up by viruses. The results produced by our computer brains most often are dictated by the quality of information that is programmed into them. Similarly, what we feed into our minds regularly will impact the thoughts and actions produced by it.

Need more evidence? A recent study published in the *Journal of Personality and Social Psychology* tracked the lives of 660 residents of a small Ohio town since 1975. The results found that those who had positive attitudes about aging lived seven-and-a-half-years longer than those who held negative views. Those who held the positive views were also happier and more energetic.[25] Of course, someone like George Burns never needed this empirical evidence.

Our beliefs have power, incredible power. Instead of computer output, our minds produce actions that are dictated in part by our belief systems. Those belief systems that help determine our actions are produced by rules that we have *artificially constructed*! That's right, these belief systems are not ingrained programs etched into our minds by heredity. We choose to believe what we believe. Often, we possess many weakening belief systems (viruses) that undermine our ability to take proper positive actions toward our goals. But by understanding our belief systems and exhibiting some effort, we can convert lame thoughts into powerful sets of positive beliefs that place virtually no limits on the possibilities we can accomplish.

There is a story about the psychotic patient with multiple personalities who regularly visits his psychiatrist. After months of therapy and discussion, the doctor was encouraged by his patient's progress. After being satisfied that the patient now only identified with only one personality, the doctor declared, "Congratulations, I believe you're cured!"

"Oh, great," the patient grimaced, obviously disappointed with the news.

"What's the matter?" the doctor said. "I thought you would be happy knowing that you no longer have delusions of being other people other than yourself."

The patient responded, "Well, six months ago I was Napoléon Bonaparte. Now I'm nobody!"

Beliefs have power. If you don't *believe* that, think about it the next time you meet somebody who thinks they are something they're not! People believe what they choose to believe and a vital step to take before pursuing our goals is actually convincing ourselves we can achieve them.

Brian Tracy, a best-selling author and self-improvement business trainer, outlines this principle in something called the "Law of Self-Expectation." Tracy states that we do not get what we want out of life. We *never* get what we want. We get what we expect.[26] Think about that for a moment. Have you ever been on a golf course where an amateur golfer hits the ball directly into a pond or into the woods and immediately exclaims, "I knew I was going to do that!"? Well, if they knew it, why did they do it? Is it possible that they feared and *expected* the ball to slice into the pond or hook into the woods? Even though they may just be a recreational hacker and not a skilled golfer, based upon that "negative" expectation, their mind could only concentrate on how *not to do it* rather than focus on the correct way.

The power of the mind

Success is 99 percent failure.—Soichiro Honda, founder, Honda Motor Corporation

Our minds are God-created—perfect intellectual computers that do what they are instructed. If we expect a certain result from our actions, usually that is what we receive. Our powerful mind machine is working constantly to pursue what it is told. The mind is like a magnet. It attracts what it concentrates on. If we want to change the results in our lives, we have to alter what information we feed into it. Remember "Garbage In, Garbage Out." If the subconscious mind is told to seek the answer of a difficult question, it will immediately begin clicking through its circuits to do so. And unless it is instructed not to, it will continue to search every cell of information stored in our cranium's long-term memory. Have you ever been searching your mind for the name of a particular movie or television actor? You say to a friend, "I know the name, it's right on the tip of my tongue!" After several frustrating attempts by the conscious mind to extract the information from the billions of information chambers in your head, you say, "Well, it will come to me." You then resume the conversation with your friend and five minutes later while in the middle of talking about a completely unrelated subject, you shout out, "Ricardo Montalban! That's the name of the guy on 'Fantasy Island!'" You are so excited that your subconscious mind kept looking for the information, even after you consciously concentrated on a totally different topic. This is no accident. This is the subconscious mind at work.

Author Gini Graham Scott writes that if the subconscious is told to stop attempting to discover a solution to an issue because the conscious mind has been convinced that an answer is impossible, the subconscious will give up.[27] Our subconscious mind does not have complete free will. That is why hypnotism is often effective. If the conscious mind can be diverted, the totally subservient subconscious will follow you like a lost puppy. Let's make this irreplaceable servant work for us. It will aid us if we ask it.

We will notice that in our own life this phenomenon of the "mind magnet" that attracts what it dwells upon. Thoughts of loneliness usually result in more isolation. Thoughts of poverty attract additional hardship. Conversely, thoughts of connection with others eventually lead to contentment and fulfilling relationships. Thoughts of prosperity held onto long enough will lead to greater wealth.

Journalist Napoleon Hill in the first part of the twentieth century studied this "Law of Attraction." Hill was commissioned by steel-magnate Andrew Carnegie for a research project to find out what made successful people, well, successful. Out of the twenty-year effort of interviewing the top performers of his day, which included Henry Ford and Alexander Graham Bell, among others, came Hill's classic book *Think and Grow Rich*. This work is a must read for anyone who wants to improve their performance in life. Among the many findings Hill discovered was the power of mind attraction. "The subconscious mind takes any orders given it in a spirit of absolute faith," Hill wrote, "and acts upon those orders, although the orders often have to be presented *over and over again*, through repetition, before they are interpreted by the subconscious mind."[28] In other words, in order to discover a solution to our problems or find what path to take to reach our desired goals, our subconscious minds must be employed. Once the message is continually fed into the subconscious mind, soon the answers start spilling out.

Before we chase after our dreams, we must have the belief to accomplish our goals and reach our destination. Then, our mental dynamo subconscious will figure out what we must do to get there. In other words, first we get it, and then it gets us.

We must also create a belief that negative results are not failure. It took Thomas Edison, the world's most prolific inventor, thousands of experiments before he successfully invented the storage battery. After the multitude of attempts that resulted in "failure," a friend of Edison's wanted to offer his condolences. To his friend's surprise, Edison reportedly replied, "Why, man, I've got a lot of results. I know several thousand things that won't work!"[29] Edison's belief in his ultimate success and views of his "results" teach us a lot about what we ordinarily define as success and failure.

Colonel Harland Sanders, the southern gentleman who after retiring in his sixties concluded that Social Security was not enough to live on, decided to see if he could sell his southern-fried chicken recipe to a restaurant. He went from eatery to eatery hawking his secret herb formula, and was repeatedly turned down by chefs and restaurant owners. It took the old Colonel scores of attempts before he had someone take him up on his offer.[30] In addition to incredible persistence, this shows that the bearded old man in the white suit became a millionaire because he believed he could succeed. He redefined the word "failure" to mean "undesired result, so try again."

The concept of failure as we know it is a disempowering belief that halts our efforts to reach our goals and deepest desires. But we can defeat limiting thoughts and substitute expanded positive beliefs with some effort. Using the influences of pleasure and pain, motivational speaker and author Anthony Robbins offers a four-step formula for changing our powerless beliefs and substituting "empowering belief systems." The formula includes identifying our disempowering belief, linking pain to that belief, creating a new positive belief, and then attaching massive pleasure to the new belief.[31]

First, we need to identify and recognize the negative beliefs that impede us. Let's search within ourselves and find a belief that has held us back. Maybe it was a belief that we cannot get promoted, find a new relationship, or master a new skill or talent. When I was beginning to write magazine articles in college I felt that I was not talented enough for any periodical to accept my work. I put all my stock in a past "failure" by a magazine not responding to a written pitch for an article. It turned out that the magazine's non-response was the result of a fire in their editorial offices and they misplaced my solicitation. A year later they wanted to publish my article, but in the time before computer disks, I had already thrown it away in frustration.

Second, as Robbins suggests, link pain to that limiting thought. We must remember the forces of pain and pleasure. Our minds will do anything to avoid pain and do just about everything to move toward pleasure. We must take our disempowering beliefs and attach massive emotional pain to them. Let's ask ourselves, what will happen if I do not change this belief? Will I always stay stuck in a dead-end job? Will I always have unsatisfying personal relationships? Is accomplishing skillful achievements only for others and not me? For myself, I remembered the frustration of giving up on my writing because I believed I could not succeed. That was painful, and I vowed never to give up again.

Next, since we disbanded our negative belief, our minds have plenty of room for a new one. Therefore, we can create a new belief. If that is so, we might as well keep a positive belief in our minds than a negative one. In order to move positively toward our objectives, we must adopt a mind-set that contains successful belief systems. Create a new belief. Say, "Yes, I can get that new job. Yes, I will have a perfect emotional relationship. Yes, I will learn to be an expert in the activities I want to pursue." Do we need documented empirical evidence that we will get the job, get the girl/guy, or truly be there and do that? Of course not! Our minds did not ask us for evidence when we said we *couldn't* accomplish those goals. Remember that the subconscious mind has no independent control! We need to tell it what we want! It will do anything we ask!

And *finally*, the last step in Robbin's formula is to attach massive pleasure to our new belief. Though affirmations are important when trying to reverse past negative thinking, affirmations alone will not succeed. After the novelty of saying, "I think I can, I think I can, I think I can" runs out of steam, we must have new fuel. That is why we need to link incredible benefits that we will gain when we adopt our new belief system. We need to tell ourselves how wonderful it will be when we get the job or promotion we want. Let's fantasize how splendid that relationship with that special person will be when we find it. Why not picture ourselves performing that desired activity flawlessly as people we respect applaud us for our talent and effort? Let's do what it takes to convince our subconscious mind that all the effort that is necessary to power our goal train over the hill will be worth it!

A major obstacle that we face in this game of life is the set of rules we play by. Most often, they are not burdensome statutes ordered by monolithic governments that restrict us. They are not laws decreed from a spiritual authority that bind our actions. Rather, they are the rules that we set up for ourselves. They are onerous regulations designed by us, often making the game impossible to win.

One example of these rules is our negative self-talk. This psychobabble issued by our pathetic inner voice says:

- *"I can't do that."*
- *"I don't deserve this."*
- *"I must be doing something wrong."*
- *"If this is working out, someone else must be the cause of it."*
- *"Whatever happens, it's probably my fault."*
- *"I can never be as good at this as they are."* Etc., etc., etc.

Our chatterbox brains, as well as naysayers around us, tell us a thousand reasons why we cannot accomplish our goals, and there are few voices in our rooting section. With this type of opposition, it is like we are a football quarterback calling signals for our team in the opponent's stadium with 80,000 fans screaming at the top of their lungs against us. We set ourselves up for defeat and often throw interceptions as a result. Then, the devil on our shoulder says, "See, I told you so!"

I liked the car commercials a few years ago for a new line of cars that unveiled a radically different series of automobiles that were totally foreign to people's previous perceptions of the carmaker. Remember, "The Rules Have Changed?" That is exactly what we must do in our lives. We have to change the rules in our favor in order to win the game. And changing the rules does not mean cheating against others. It is simply "leveling the playing field" in our own minds. Let's give at least equal time, if not all the time, to the Thomas Edison voice inside of us that says:

- *"I can do it."*

- *"Yes, I'm proud of that accomplishment, I worked very hard on it."*

- *"I know it is a big dream, but others have done so by applying their skills and effort and so can I."*

- *"It didn't work out this time, but my effort was not a failure, it was only an undesired result, and I'll try again in different ways until I achieve success."*

We must believe a positive premise if we are going to defeat our opponents: negativity, disappointment, and naysaying. If we change the rules upon which we build our house of goals, we will change our life. Remember, "Anything the mind can conceive and believe, it can achieve."

OPPORTUNITY:

Write down three negative beliefs that are holding you back. Attach a painful thought to them. Next to each, write a positive belief and a pleasurable feeling that can propel you forward.

1.

2.

3.

6

Goals—The Blueprint for Action

Success equals goals: All else is commentary.—Brian Tracy

Some research studies suggest that the average income for those individuals who set specific *written* goals for themselves is significantly higher than those who do not set specific objectives. That appears to be common sense. I submit to you that the lion's share of those who have a clear picture of where they want to go in life usually end up there. Those who do not have clear goals end up someplace they did not imagine. I am convinced that young people who have written goals for their life will not only be better off financially later on in life, but also have a more stable family structure, be more socially adjusted, be more involved in their communities, and will consider themselves happier than persons who have no specific written goals. Motivational expert Zig Ziglar contends that most people give up what they want *most* for what they want *now.* Instant gratification again wins out over planning and patience. Most people think of the now and do not plan for the future. Many critics of our sometimes increasingly hedonistic society cite the sense of "immediate gratification" as a major culprit to our lack of vision. Many studies reveal that people prefer single desirable actions in the immediate rather than the distant future, and the fruits of which are increasingly positive or decreasingly negative.[32] Researchers argue that the ability to avoid the need for immediate gratification to earn long-term results reflects a basic social and cognitive competence.[33] Are we willing to sacrifice what we want now for what we want most? If we are forming brand new goals, author and public speaker Roger Dawson suggests: look back to our childhood to find what we were good at then; find what we perceive as play, not work; and pose the question: what would we do with our lives if we were assured of success?[34] Are we willing to write our plan for the future?

Writing about exciting life goals has been shown to have health benefits as well. Disclosive writing about life-upsetting events has been cited by a number of studies as serving as an emotional release and catharsis. However, a study by Southern Methodist University found that "writing about life goals was significantly *less upsetting* [italics mine] than writing about trauma and was associated with a *significant increase* [ditto] in subjective well being" without the emotional costs.[35]

This evidence reveals that written goals are powerful. And whether we realize it or not, everyone has goals, though they may not be written. But writing goals down is powerful. As the saying goes, the faintest ink is stronger than the best memory. All human goals are created equal, but to play on words from George Orwell's novel *Animal Farm,* "Some goals are more equal than others." Our goals may be to roll out of bed in the morning, avoid facing the wrath of the boss, getting the kids to bed before we blow a gasket from exhaustion, etc. But man and woman do not live by routine pleasure-seeking, pain-avoiding, and immediate-gratification goals alone. We need inspirational goals that motivate us to consistent action for the prize in the future. And we should *write* them down.

Those who possess invigorating goals are excited about life, are rarely bored, and deal with adversity better than those who are simply meandering through their daily existence. Those who have energized objectives take responsibility for their actions and evaluate the results they achieve from those efforts. Those who do not set clear, positive goals usually deny accountability for their actions and often blame others for their own failures.

Imagine a football team taking the field without well-designed plays, hours of difficult practice, and a confident teamwork attitude. The team is likely to be a loser. The disgruntled players will complain about the officials' incompetence and lack of fairness, the coach would grumble about the players' lack of commitment, and the team owner may fire the coach. Few would confess that they shared in the responsibility for the poor play. This does not mean if we do not have specific goals written down on paper, we are inferior or incompetent people. Of course not. But, if we do choose to cite specific goals in our lives that are in alignment with our value structure and are in harmony with our stated purpose for living, we do not have time to point the fingers at others for dropping the ball. We are busy huddling up for the next play or practice. In the next game, we are more confident that we will be successful.

People with ambitious goals can hardly contain their thrill about pursuing their objectives. Many people without goals are not nearly as excited about their prospects in life. That does not mean they are boring people. It only means they have impotent goals. Goals do not have to be profound, earth-shattering accomplishments that will turn the tide of humanity. They can be simple, yet very important to us as well as others. A goal could be to live as a caring parent, a loving spouse, or a generous person. I believe those goals do the world a lot more good than inventing the next electronic gadget that can make us see through steel walls. But whatever our goals are, they must be exciting and important enough to give us the necessary fuel to blast out of the gravity of the "negative forces" that often restrain our launch. Who are these nasty beasties? They are *fear, worry, guilt, low self-esteem, ignorant apathy,* and *responsibility avoidance.*

Why Don't People Have Exciting Goals?

To conquer fear is the beginning of wisdom.—Bertrand Russell

1. FEAR

We may have heard that the word **FEAR** is an acronym for a number of phrases such as *False Evidence Appearing Real* or *Forget Everything and Run*. Fear's twin offspring *Worry* and *Guilt* are two non-productive emotions that cannot change the past, do not contribute to the present, and impede development in the future. And they often keep us from our goals.

How do we dispel fear, worry, and guilt? Well, easier said than done. Thousands of psychologists make an affluent living helping their patients deal with their fears. And there are real fears. Fear is a survival response in human beings to keep us alive. We know that real fear is being in the road in front of an oncoming automobile. We know that real fear is crossing the path of two muggers in the night on an abandoned street. These "real" fears are good fears that trigger our fight-or-flight syndrome. They keep us safe and alive. However, most fears that prevent us from setting and achieving goals are representative as the first acronym FEAR—*False Evidence Appearing Real.* Most fears are, in fact, false. President Franklin Delano Roosevelt told the American people during the Great Depression that, "We have nothing to fear, but fear itself." That is not only true in times of despair, but also it is accurate when we are hesitant to map out our goals.

Chemist Marie Curie said, "Nothing in life is to be feared, only understood." If we understand which fears are true, and which are false, it can act as an impetus for action toward our goals. False fears prevent action, instead of acting as a catalyst for performance. That is the key. We must understand our fears. When we reach this level of comprehension we will know which fear to take seriously and which fear we can ignore.

False fear is the opposite of our goals. Dr. Denis Waitley, author of *Psychology of Winning* and numerous other motivational books, agrees that we must be aware that fear and desire drive motivation. Waitley says, "Winners are driven by desire." We move in the direction of what we dwell upon. While both fear and desire motivate, it is obvious that fear will drive us away from our goals.[36]

Likewise, management-trainer Brian Tracy suggests we conquer our fears by:

- Act as if the thing we fear does not exist;

- Do what we fear;

- Confront our fears; and

- Make of habit of doing it. Accept the risk.[37]

Dr. Susan Jeffries, in her book *Feel the Fear and Do It Anyway*, gives suggestions in dealing with fear by realizing that:

- The problems won't go away;

- When we do what we fear, we feel better;

- Everyone else is not better at it that we are; and

- Pushing through our fear is easier than dealing with the helplessness we feel because of it.[38]

Mark Sanborn, author of *High Impact Leadership*, suggests not concentrating on how we feel facing our fears, but rather, how do we feel if we *do not* take that challenge? Fear robs us of the power we need to achieve our goals. If you have certain fears that have prevented you from setting and pursuing goals, list them. The first step towards personal change, leadership expert Blaine Lee writes in his book *The Power Principle*, is "awakening" that leads to awareness, choice, decision, and eventually, taking a leap of faith.[39] Identify your fears and then seek to understand them.

OPPORTUNITY:

List the major fears that you experience in your life. Then identify them as either real or imagined fears. If they are imagined, what do you have to fear?

As for worry and guilt, I'm not concerned and I'm not sorry about it. Seriously, what does worry about the future and guilt regarding the past provide us? Stress? Ulcers? Headaches? Depression? It sure does not provide results toward our goals. It has been said that 90 percent of the things we worry about never happen, and the other 10 percent we cannot control anyway. It is easier said than done to say, "don't worry, be happy" and "don't feel guilty" even though we may share responsibility. We must first realize that no matter how real those emotions are, they provide nothing of value to us.

Instead of worrying, think of positive outcomes. They have more of a chance to occur if we take assertive action than negative ones. Again, if we feel positive thinking alone does not work, what does worry alone accomplish? Poet Robert Frost said, "The reason why worry kills more people than work is that more people worry than work." Let's stop worrying. Let's start working toward our goals. In lieu of guilt, remember that responsibility teaches us a lesson to take corrective action in the future. The past is over. Learn from it, but don't dwell on it.

2. Low Self-esteem

This is a real killer. We have heard that low self-esteem is said to be behind reasons for inner-city crime, pregnant teenagers, and trips to the psychologist. We know the terms: low self-image; low self-appreciation; and the lack of self-confidence. Many times we feel unworthy of the dreams we form in our minds. We are not good enough, not talented enough, not rich enough, not tough enough, not smart enough, etc., etc., etc. True self-confidence is not inbred in us like the courage of a lion. It is learned. Lack of self-confidence is embedded into our minds at a very early age. The good news is it can be unlearned.

Dr. Martin Seligman's book *Learned Optimism* is chock full of research involving how people actually learn to be *helpless!* Dr. Seligman, a professor of psychology at the University of Pennsylvania and past president of the American Psychological Association, explains that experiments with animals showed that once an animal is conditioned to believe that it cannot achieve a desired goal (e.g., reach a plate of food behind a barrier), it continued to refuse to reach that objective even though the barrier was removed. This is similar to the "Invisible Fence" concept many use to keep their pets from roaming off their property. Seligman asserts that human beings are no different. In a subsequent work, *Authentic Happiness*, Seligman states that the best way to defeat pessimistic thinking is by first recognizing and then actively disputing negative thoughts in our minds.[40] If we are convinced by others, or convince ourselves that we cannot achieve a goal, we will be reluctant to attempt it. Remember Henry Ford? "Whether you believe you can or you believe you can't, you're right!"

The questions our chatterbox brains constantly ask us set us up for defeat and deliver blows to our self-esteem. We must understand the power of these questions. When we look in the mirror to see a few extra pounds that have crept up on us over the holiday do we ask:

A. "Why am I so fat?" or

B. "How can I eat better foods, increase the level of exercise in my life, and still find it pleasurable?"

Our minds will give an answer to both questions. To the first negative question, it will answer, "Because you eat too much and are too lazy to exercise! So don't even bother—get another cookie!" To the second more positive and constructive query the mind may respond, "Hey, you can join a weight loss group with your friends and you can start playing in a volleyball league at the YMCA. That would be a blast!"

The results in our lives will be largely determined by the questions we feed into our minds. As Wally Amos, creator of the Famous Amos cookies once claimed, "Happiness is an inside job." Whenever we ask a question, we receive an answer. So let's ask quality and positive-oriented questions.

3. Ignorant Apathy

This is the "I don't know and I don't care" philosophy. Many of us ignore goal-setting because we have no idea what our potential for success is. We feel that the social class our family belongs to, the neighborhood we live in, the financial condition of our parents, or the level of education we received as a child carves our course in life into a permanent dead-end track. Or apathy has set in—that dangerous creeping disease that paralyzes our actions. We conclude that our main goal in life to not miss our favorite soap opera, or make sure there is enough beer in the refrigerator for the big game. Or perhaps our lust for life is dwindling due to family commitments, financial pressures, or stress. We once were in a groove and now it has become a rut.

We had passion, hope, fantasies, dreams, and aspirations in our youth. But we are older and wiser now. We have been there and done that. We tried it that way and it does not work. It was only naiveté and the foolishness of immaturity that made us believe we could reach our dreams. Turn on the TV, crack open a beer and a bag of chips, put our brains on hold, and let's find more temporary, hypnotic, and excessive mind-numbing pleasures churned out by Hollywood so as not to remind us of either where we are or where we are *not* going.

Ignorant apathy. There is an easy cure. Imagine as much as we can and care as much as we can imagine. Do not tune into the tube, tune into yourself. There lies more exciting drama (and comedy!) than we could find on any stage or movie theater. It is projected in 3-D video and surround-sound audio. And it is more genuine than virtual reality. It is called life!

4. Lack of Responsibility

The late Latin comedian Freddie Prinze, star of the 1970s TV-series *Chico and the Man*, was known for his signature line when confronted with a problem: "Eezze not my job, man." Though said in jest, that is exactly what many of us say when things do not turn out the way we intended. From the four-year-old boy who breaks a living room lamp and blames a monster to the corporate board members pointing fingers at the vice-president of accounting for financial shenanigans; and, from the divorcing couple waging a domestic war through attorneys to the top seats of government condemning another branch of government for a failure of policy, we have become a nation full of blame-making children, refusing to take responsibility for our own actions. We sometimes fear responsibility because we perceive it to be accepting blame, criticism, punishment, or penalties for our good-faith actions.

Responsibility is not blame, however. It is a ticket to freedom. By taking responsibility, we are saying that we are in charge of our actions. And if we achieve less-than-desired results, we know that we are in control of how to improve our methods the next time we confront a similar problem or face another comparable opportunity. We are not perfect; we are human. But to be mature human beings, we must be accountable for the results of our actions. But we cannot take responsibility for everything, we may say. For example, are we answerable if lightning strikes us? Is that not an act of God? Yes, perhaps, but we should take responsibility for walking in the rain wearing a metal hat and steel-toed shoes! Seriously, we are not always at fault for actions occurring to us, but we are always in control of our reaction to those events.

Whatever happens in our life, we need to take responsibility for our *reactions*. The Greek philosopher Epictetus said, "People are troubled not by things themselves, but how they interpret them." Or as Shakespeare wrote in Hamlet, "There is nothing either good or bad, but thinking makes it so." Our reactions will determine how successful we are in rebounding from any temporary setback. Our calculated response to a sudden opportunity will put us far ahead than an ingrained reactive answer programmed into us by negative past experiences. We can rehearse our positive reactions in life. If we expect opposition as we pursue our goals, we can map out a battle plan to confront life's unexpected twists and turns.

Those who are in control of their lives and take responsibility of what their minds concentrate on not only have a greater ability to reach their goals, but also have the capability of surviving extreme adversity. We have heard of the wondrous stories of people trapped by snowstorms, mine collapses, or other natural disasters, who endured extreme temperatures or plight because they kept their minds focused on survival, not defeat. Everyone knows the story of Private Jessica Lynch, seriously abused by her Iraqi captors in 2003, who was near the point of hopelessness and certain death. But her faith in rescue most likely kept her alive until fellow soldiers arrived. "I just wanted to look up and see a soldier standing there at the foot of my bed," she said. As reporter Rick Bragg wrote, "She scripted it in her mind. She would open her eyes and he would be there, and he would say that he had come to take her home."[41] Those who have the highest concentration on their goals can survive the most atrocious oppression imaginable.

During psychologist Viktor Frankl's experience in the Auschwitz "death factory," he observed human behavior under the most terrible of circumstances. Frankl was a determinist raised in the Freudian psychology tradition of blaming your adult character on your traumatic childhood experiences. After incarceration with virtually no hope of release and experiencing unspeakable, inhuman degradation, Frankl theorized that even under the most brutal of circumstances, man *does* have a choice of action. In his narrative *Man's Search for Meaning*, the author states that some prisoners, despite being treated worse than animals by the Nazis, gave away their last piece of bread to others to comfort their suffering. This, Frankl states, offers "sufficient proof that everything can be taken from a man but one thing: the last of the human freedoms—to choose one's attitude in any given set of circumstances, to choose one's own way."[42] In other words, our spiritual inner-freedom of choice can never be imprisoned and is the key to drawing meaning from life. As stated earlier, Frankl found that the prisoners who were able to concentrate on their potential life after the concentration camp (i.e., goals) had a better chance of enduring the callous treatment of the Nazis. Frankl found that no matter how many dignities the Nazis took away, they could not control what a person thought about. That is entirely up to the individual.

Despite the opposition we face in our lives, not much can compare with being a prisoner of war or an inmate in a concentration camp. By accepting responsibility for our reactions to events by focusing on solutions, not the problems, we can overcome nearly any adversity. One common "excuse" for not taking on new goals, or conquering old ones, is the defense of "I'm too old," or "It's too late now." It is only too late if we have decided to quit.

Former National Football League quarterback Frank Reich is not a household sports name like Hall of Fame quarterbacks John Elway or Dan Marino. But Reich holds two precious achievements as a quarterback that may never be equaled. In January 1992, the Buffalo Bills faced the Houston Oilers in a Wild Card Playoff game at Rich Stadium in Orchard Park, New York. The Bills, American Football Conference Champions for the previous two years, were vying to reach the Super Bowl for the third year in a row, an awesome feat, in itself. However, things did not go well for the Bills in the first half of the game. Houston pummeled Buffalo in the first thirty minutes of the contest and led the defending conference champions at halftime by the score of 28—3. To add injury to insult, the Bills pro-bowl quarterback, Jim Kelly, was out of the game with a serious injury. It was a bitter cold day in Buffalo, and despite the normal zealous support for their football team, thousands of fans left the stands figuring that it was over and went home to get warm.

Kelly's understudy, Frank Reich, who had spent most of his professional football career carrying a clipboard on the sidelines rather than a football in the backfield, refused to give in. On the first series of plays in the second half, Reich stepped back to pass and let the ball go. It was a completion—to the wrong team. Houston intercepted the pass and ran for a touchdown. The score was now 35—3, less than a half to play. "It's all over for Buffalo," said the game's television announcers. More people left the stands. Many more Bills fans outside the home market watching the game on television flicked off their TV sets. Frank Reich could have said, "Well, we are too far behind, anyway. It isn't my fault. It's too late now. It's not my responsibility." That is where things became interesting.

Reich, who had little playing time behind the future Hall-of-Famer Kelly, did not look as if he could help the floundering Bills. But the second-string QB, a deeply religious person with plenty of faith, refused to surrender. Few knew that Reich possessed a *college* football record. While playing for the University of Maryland Terrapins, Reich was, you guessed it, a back-up quarterback. During one game, the Terrapins were being dismembered by the mighty Miami Hurricanes by the score of 31-0 by halftime. With nothing to lose, Reich was called in to quarterback the second half. With strong belief in what he could do, Reich mastered the greatest comeback in *college* football history and won the game.

With that evidence of past achievement and faith in his abilities and confidence of his team behind him, Reich took the responsibility of the mistake of the second half's first pass against Houston. Then, the no-name back-up quarterback marched the Bills into the end zone time after time and the Bills won the game in overtime by a score of 41—38, the greatest comeback in *professional* football history. The underdog Bills won the next two playoff games and went to the Super Bowl for the third straight year.

This story is not just an anecdote for the sports world. It is for everyone who is tempted to rationalize explanations. Instead, set challenging goals, focus on objectives, and take action. It is never too late to pursue our goals. Accept no excuses. Take responsibility. Reach back and let the ball fly!

Juggling Act—Balancing our Roles and Goals

My father said I should be a lawyer. 'You could get a little something for yourself.' Then my mother said no, no, no, he should be an author, he should write books. 'That's a good life, you could get a little something for yourself.' But what they didn't understand was that I wanted everything.—Bruce Springsteen

No matter how old a person lives, if they feel they have not accomplished their "mission" here on earth, they regret their life may soon be over with their job left "undone." On the other hand, we have seen the lives of many great people who have died very young, who could have accomplished even greater feats in their futures if they only survived. But as you examine those remarkable individuals who were cut down by assassins in our lifetime, like John and Robert Kennedy, Martin Luther King, Jr., Anwar Sadat, Yitzhak Rabin, John Lennon, etc., you see that their life did have great meaning. Their lives, though short by today's expected life-expectancy standards, touched many people and literally changed the world. Though those celebrated persons had many goals in mind, we see that the pursuit of their "purpose" was the important quest that is their legacy.

Conversely, many people who achieve great honors and live many years may end up bitter and unsatisfied. Ty Cobb, one of the greatest hitters and base stealers in professional baseball, attained more records than anyone did in his time. Yet, Cobb, as it turned out, was an acrimonious and lonely man who said late in life that if he had to live his life over again he would "have more friends." He did not say more hits, or steals, or money, or women. He said, "more friends."

What this says to us is that no matter how many goals we put on our plates, we must present a balanced meal. We cannot concentrate solely on one aspect of our lives, though that may be our natural strong point. We have many roles to fulfill and we must attain some level of homeostasis, or *balance*. We may fulfill a function of businessperson. But we also may play a critical role as a parent. Perhaps we have adopted a well-defined responsibility as a spouse. But we also live the life as a spiritual follower of God. We may work out at the gym daily to keep our bodies in shape, but we also need to exercise and stretch our minds on a regular basis. We probably perform a dozen roles every single week such as Little League coach, caring parent, church leader, grocery shopper, meal planner, caregiver to an elderly parent, and being an ear to a friend in trouble. But we need equilibrium in our lives so all of our roles and goals do not come tumbling down because of a break in one link of the chain.

Do you remember the children's game "Don't Break the Ice?" The object of the game was to take a plastic hammer and punch out ice blocks on an elevated game board. Each player would continue to punch out ice blocks until all the blocks fell sending a little man on top tumbling below. The game's players could knock out many blocks of ice, and if they were strategically selected, the man would remain standing. The concept worked because no one block was responsible for holding the man up and one block could fall without the entire structure collapsing.

The balance of our roles and goals in life can work the same way. If we put all of our stock, goals, and concentration into only *one* of our roles in our life, imagine what would happen if life's hammer would come and smash our one block. Instead of a small piece tumbling to the ground, down would come our entire effort, leaving us depleted, devastated, and depressed.

All of the roles of our life are important. Some deserve more attention than others do at times, but none can be neglected for extended periods. For example, if we have a new baby in our household, our role as a parent dominates our life from 3 a.m. feedings to doctor visits for the infant. Where we can go, what we can do, and when we can do it is controlled by that little helpless creature! But, I am sure we will recognize that after a while, we have to start looking out for ourselves as well, for our health, our careers, and our sanity!

The key is *identifying* our most important goals in the various roles we have in our daily life and then prioritizing them. The power of goal-setting is phenomenal and the charge it gives us when we map out our objectives juices us up with more energy than we have ever experienced. But we must be careful. If we load our plate up with too many goals in too many roles, we can end up crashing down from the weight of our own dreams.

I found out this personally. After taking time to see what my purpose was in life, defining my primary principles, my most vital values, and my daring dreams, I jumped in with both feet to pursue numerous goals in many roles of my life. I had a goal to be a positive role model for my children by spending a great deal of time and attention with them. Since I was single at the time, I sought a goal of a satisfying relationship with the woman I began dating. I also pursued my dream of being a writer by beginning the novel I always wanted to start, but never found time to write. I returned to school to obtain a Masters degree to further my career in business. I was involved in research of self-development material and was developing my own workshop on the subject. I rejuvenated my interest in music and practiced the piano and guitar on a daily basis. I began reading much more and listening to audiotapes in the car. I increased my responsibilities in the community by volunteer work for various agencies and activity in my church. I was learning a foreign language for a possible trip to Europe. I stepped up my exercise regimen by running, swimming, biking, and weight lifting. I took skiing lessons, ballroom dance lessons, and various other group activities for fun and health. I discovered the power of goal-setting that aligned activities and objectives with my principles and values. However, I found that, unfortunately, I was only one person. Overload, burnout, stress, and less-than-desired results in some of the areas occurred. I learned that with the power of goal-setting I could do *anything* I wanted. But, I also discovered that I could not do *everything* I wanted.

I demonstrate this concept for others by attempting to juggle four tennis balls. I give one tennis ball to someone and ask him or her to throw it to me when I say, "now." Then, I begin to juggle the three remaining balls. After juggling the three for a few seconds, I say "now!" The assistant throws the fourth ball to me and all the tennis balls fall to the floor. After I glower at my helper I ask him or her, "Do you know why I dropped all the balls?" The embarrassed person usually says they threw the ball to me "too high, too low, too fast, or too slow." Then, I say, "No. The reason I dropped all the balls is that I don't know how to juggle *four* balls!"

If we try to juggle too many goals in various roles we are likely to see many of our newfound or rediscovered aspirations tumble. We should start out with just one primary goal in our various life roles. After a while, we many be able to juggle two. But, if we concentrate on just one, the most important one, we are likely to see positive results that will continue to be a perpetual fire to fuel our desire to accomplish more.

Prioritization. Balance. Focus. Those are the things we must keep in mind in goal-setting. There are virtually no limits to the types of goals we can pursue. However, once we come up with plenty of ideas to push toward, we must then fine-tune our goals by ranking them in importance to our mission. We must also not overload one role of our lives at the expense of the others that are also significant to us. Our goals must be prioritized. Our roles must be balanced. Then we can focus and stay on track on our own determined purpose. Stephen Covey puts prioritization of our mission, roles, and goals this way in his book, *First Things First*: "The main thing is to keep the main thing, the main thing."[43] Can we keep the main thing the main thing? It is a challenge, but yes we can.

OPPORTUNITY:

What is the main thing in your life that you should be focusing on right now?

7

Brainstormy Weather—The Goal Creation Process

What imagination seizes as Beauty must be truth—whether it existed before or not.—John Keats

Now comes the fun part of goal-setting! This is the time to let our imagination fly! This is the opportunity to recapture our youth and think like a kid again! We are going brainstorming!

We have all probably brainstormed before and probably do it everyday but do not realize it. There are some basic rules that we must follow:

- *First*, in order to brainstorm for ideas of potential goals, we first need a brain. Unless we are an unconfident scarecrow, chances are we qualify. Size does not matter. If we have convoluted gray matter somewhere in our head, we fit the bill.

- *Second*, when conjuring up a brain blizzard, we must accept that *anything goes*. Any idea that floats through our minds, we must write it down. It does not matter how far-fetched the idea is, or how impractical it may seem right now. From crazy propositions come tomorrow's realities. Write down whatever comes to mind. Often, unrealistic concepts generate other pragmatic ideas that we may never have considered without the outlandish thought occurring first.

- *Third*, we *cannot* judge any idea during brainstorming. During this exercise, *quantity* is much more important than *quality*. When we come up with a possible goal, the programmed "negative" tendency of our reactive mind is to shoot our ideas full of holes before they even get off the ground. We must resist the temptation to do that. We will go through a process later of prioritizing our goals and evaluating whether they are truly aligned with our purpose. But, at this point, we must crank out ideas faster than we ever have before.

- *Fourth*, this process should only last ten to fifteen minutes at most. We can always add possible goals to our list as they come to us later. But we must first come up with a good list to move to the next step. We could end up brainstorming for weeks and then be too exhausted to start taking action on anything.

- *Finally*, we must approach the brainstorming process with incredible power. "Act as if you could not fail," suggests Dr. Robert Schuller, the noted positive-thinking author and television minister in discussing his concept of "possibility thinking."[44] We must set goals with the mind-set that finances are of no concern, current obligations have no bearing, age does not matter, current knowledge is inconsequential, and time is no object.

On the following page is an example of different types of roles we may have in our life. We may have some of the roles, and not others. We may have other roles that are not even listed. This is only a guide to get us started. We may list only one goal in a particular role, or we may list a dozen. At this point, it does not matter.

Let's begin listing our goals and keep extra copies as we should periodically brainstorm again to come up with more ideas. The goal areas are divided into four categories:

1. *Spiritual and Social Goals,*

2. *Growth Goals,*

3. *Contribution Goals,* and

4. *Physical or Material Goals.*

Notice that this roughly corresponds with the four basic human needs referred to earlier. Under each category are examples of the various roles we have already identified in our lives. I have given examples of some basic goals for explanation purposes. Please develop *your own* in the upcoming brainstorming OPPORTUNITY.

Underneath **Spiritual and Social Goals**:

- *Spiritual bonding with God* (attending church, temple, or a mosque regularly, joining a prayer or devotion group, reading spiritual literature or meditating);

- *Family and intimate relationships* (being a supportive wife or husband, taking the kids out on family trips, calling a sibling we haven't spoken to in a while, listening to our friends' concerns); and

- *Social activity* (joining a card club, attending dances, taking in a movie with our friends on a regular basis);

Listed below are **Growth Goals**:

- *Personal Development* (listening to motivational tapes to become enthusiastic about goals, learning a foreign language for an upcoming vacation, building our vocabulary);

- *Career objectives* (doing more than our job requires to be considered for a promotion, marketing our resume to get a better job, taking night classes to learn new job skills); and

- *Artistic or skill-based pursuits* (reading up on a new skill, joining a choir, learning to play a musical instrument).

And under *Contribution Goals*:

- *Building goals* (becoming involved in a get-out-the-vote drive, organizing a neighborhood crime watch, helping to build a school playground); and

- *Contribution goals* (increasing our support for charitable giving, joining a service group to help the elderly, teaching children to paint at a summer camp, visiting friends in the hospital or nursing home).

Beneath *Physical and Material Goals*:

- *Diet and exercise needs* (eating more fruits and vegetables, walking briskly every day, getting enough sleep);

- *Financial health* (beginning a retirement savings program, drawing up a monthly spending plan, saving for a new house); and

- *Material items* (buying a new car, planning a trip to Europe, or starting a collection of antiques).

BIG OPPORTUNITY:

For a ten-to-fifteen minute period, brainstorm a series of possible goals under each area mentioned. If you are stumped under any area, move to the next. If an idea does not fit in a particular zone, make up your own miscellaneous category. The importance right now is the ideas, not where you are going to put them.

Remember, right now, set your sights high. From big goals come big motivations. Write down anything you have ever wanted to be, anything you have ever wanted to do, and anything you have ever wanted to have. What did you enjoy when you were a child? What would you do if you won the lottery tomorrow? What would you look like if you were in perfect physical shape? What would your relationship with your significant other be like if it were perfect? If you are not in a relationship, in your mind, describe what would a perfect relationship be like? What did you ever want to accomplish? Do you want to write a novel or go on an African safari? What would your family relationships be like if they were as enriching as you could imagine? What job would make work seem like play? What books would you read? What would you like to give back to your community? What do you want people to remember you by?

As we ask ourselves these questions, we must remember the force of these queries. We should ask positive results-oriented "what if" questions to fuel our motivation toward our goals. "What if I succeed in taking aim on a new job possibility? How would I feel?" On the other hand, strategically asked, "what if I don't" questions can also repel us from the results we do not want to see. "What if I don't take action towards my goal? How miserable will I be if I fail to take action?"

Now it is your turn. Begin the goals brainstorm. It will be a department store full of goodies you can choose from. For the next ten to fifteen minutes, unleash your wildest imagination.

My Goals: Anything I've ever wanted to be, to have, to do, or to give

Next, place your proposed goals in one of the following categories:

Spiritual/Love Goals

Spiritual

Family & Relationship

Social

Growth Goals

Personal Development

Artistic/Skill-based

Career

Contribution Goals

Building

Contribution

Physical & Material Goals

Physical

Financial

Material

Now you have a suggested list of goals. Do you have too many goals in one category? Do you lack goals in some of the categories? Rethink your possible goals. Then, in each category, prioritize the goals in order of their importance to you. Don't rank the categories against one another lest you try to compare your various goals unfairly (e.g., financial goals vs. spiritual goals). Do you see balance in your life based on your goals?

Finally, let me share with you the story of Sarah (not her real name). Sarah was a young professional who was new in a city. She was shy, unconfident in her social abilities, but very confident in her professional abilities. Because of poor experiences in the corporate work force, she vowed to start her own advertising business. But business in the new town was slow. She lacked contacts and was struggling to pay the rent. Personally, things for Sarah were even worse. She had few friends in the new town, and feared close relationships with men because she had been hurt in the past. The only romance she had in her life went sour and left a bad taste in her mouth. She was in her early forties and now felt that she was too old to start a family, though that was something she desperately wanted to do. She became overweight and ashamed of her appearance. She spent her days at her new business with little work to do and nights home alone watching TV and overeating. She was depressed and despondent.

One day, one of Sarah's few friends said she should join a local health club to work off her extra pounds. "It's a great place to meet people, too," her friend advised. After several excuses and nights worrying about the cost of a membership that she could not afford, she came to a decision to risk it. She joined the club.

Nervous, she attended the health facility for the first time. And you know what happened? Nothing. Nothing except she was embarrassed to exercise because of her bulky appearance and she could not figure out how most of the exercise equipment worked. Humiliated, she went home.

The next day, she regained her courage and went again, and guess what happened? Again, nothing. Nothing except she thought she was going to have a heart attack in the aerobic class she signed up to attend. The same results continued for a few weeks, until another person at the health club offered to help her operate a weight machine she could not figure out. The other woman, named Ann, often came to the club the same time Sarah did. After a few days, they began to talk more and exercised together. After a few more weeks, Ann invited Sarah to take in a movie with her friends. At the movie, Sarah met Debbie, who coincidentally, owned a local line of laundromats, and was looking for someone to do her advertising. Sarah got the job and things at her business picked up. Through Debbie, Sarah met Joanne, who pitched a membership in a local service club that could expand her business contacts. Sarah was still nervous about spending more money on another membership, but she was sold on joining. At the service club, Sarah met many more friends and business contacts and her business picked up new clients. She performed volunteer work with the service club at a local agency for disabled children. This expression of love for those needy kids brought new meaning into Sarah's life and she felt even greater about the health she took for granted. At the kid's agency, she met one of the organization's directors, Ron. Sandy, who had dropped some weight at the health club by working out regularly and eating right, felt better about herself. Ron, a divorced father of two, was raising his sixteen- and thirteen-year-old boys on his own. He asked Sarah out for a date. Sarah was afraid to date again at first, but after the third request, she agreed. He was kind of cute, she thought. Ron and Sarah hit it off, and within a year, the two fell in love and married. Sarah's business boomed, her health improved, she looked great, Ron was terrific, his kids loved her, and she possessed an instant family that she once thought she would never experience.

What an incredible journey for Sarah! Unbelievable story, huh? You are absolutely right! Because all of this was TOTAL FICTION. I made it up. Well, there is a professional named Sarah (not her real name) who has all the misery I outlined in the beginning of the story. But none of those other events ever happened. Why? *Because Sarah never took her friend's advice to go to the health club.* She rationalized and said it was too expensive, while the real reason was that she feared being embarrassed—a phony fear. One opportunity turned down kept the rest of the potential dominos from falling. This story may be fiction, but you know there are a million stories just like it that are absolutely true. I could tell you a dozen true stories that are just as miraculous as Sarah's fictional one. You could probably cite a few yourself. It is called life. I tell this fictional story not to fool you, but to confess that we all have Sarah inside of us. We are all Sarah at one time or another because we fear to take that first step. Remember the Chinese proverb, "The longest journey begins with a single step?" But the first step is usually the hardest. It takes courage. It takes drive. It takes a burning desire to make a critical decision to change the results in our lives and commit to that decision. It takes action! Believe me, once that first step is taken, it is much easier to take the second step. Before we know it, we are running. The exhilaration from the run focuses us and fuels us even more. By the time we are approaching the finish line of our goal, we cannot even imagine why it was so hard to take that first step.

Remember Sarah's needs, if formed with focus, could have been powerful goal motivators: Get new business and create income, form meaningful friendships, lose weight and improve health, find a nourishing relationship and form a family, give back our bounty and benefits to those who need them. All of them could have been potentially, even accidentally addressed, by only making one small decision and taking one small action. Imagine what Sarah could have done if she consciously organized her goals and took several actions and believed that she would succeed. There would be no stopping her!

8

The Goal Litmus Test—Separating the Wheat from the Chaff

Nothing endures but change.—Heraclitus

If you have completed the goal brain-blizzard, you should have a gargantuan collection of goals, wants, needs, objectives, and a Christmas list that would boggle Santa's mind. If you have not done this OPPORTUNITY, you must go back and complete it before proceeding, or the rest of the strategy will not work. You need a list of potential goals to work with.

Now that we have a slew of goals, what's next? Where do we start? Realistically, if we properly did the OPPORTUNITY, we listed enough goals for ten people to accomplish in a lifetime. How do we find the gold nugget goals in all these wishes? Well, we can apply the *Goal Litmus Test* to select the goals we will be absolutely passionate about and will bring out our true mission. Remember the juggling act I talked about? When faced with multiple goals that will lead to burnout and disaster, we need to make choices. At first it seems tough. We have just gone through an OPPORTUNITY that made us feel like a kid with a $20 bill set loose in a penny-candy store and now we have to choose whether we buy red licorice or chocolate kisses? Why rain on the parade?

The first step in narrowing down our brainstorming list is called *grouping*. As we look down our list of potential goals—some of which we may already be in the process of pursuing—we need to see if there are similar goals that could be combined with others. For example, we may have a goal to learn how to play a new musical instrument. We may also have a goal to join a choral group. Group those two ideas together and give it a subhead, like "music." By doing this, we will not be overwhelmed by a laundry list of goals that may intimidate us. If we have twenty potential goals listed under career development, we may wonder when we will ever have the time to reach them, or we may be paralyzed making a decision of what we should accomplish first. First we need to list our ideas, and then group similar ones together making it a simpler list to look at.

Second, we must *prioritize*. If we have three subheads under our financial goals, (e.g., increase savings for a home, take on a second job for extra income, and draw up a spending plan), we then must think about which is the most important to us. For example, increasing savings and earning extra income are noteworthy goals, but we may decide that the most critical thing we should do is to identify where our current funds are going! If we do that, we would rank "draw up a monthly spending plan" as number one. Accomplishing that logically leads to our other goals of earning more income and increasing our savings.

The Goal Litmus Test

Finally, let's use the power of questions again to make sure the goals we have listed are as powerful as possible. Ask the following questions:

1. Does our goal coincide with our mission?

Our life can be compared to a train's journey. We want to constantly move forward and enjoy the trip. But the tracks for our journey must bring us to a worthy destination. What good is reaching a goal if it means little to the purpose of our lives? Chapter Four talked about forming a written purpose. We should reread our purpose before beginning the planning of a goal strategy. If we have listed part of our purpose as "serving others to best of our ability," a goal of becoming executive vice president of the company we work for no matter what the cost to our fellow employees or the public may conflict with that. If we have goals that clash with our purpose, chances are we are going to have second thoughts if we follow that path.

OPPORTUNITY:

List your major goals and write a sentence emphasizing how your goal coincides with your mission.

Goal No. 1:
Why it aligns with my mission:

Goal No. 2:
Why it aligns with my mission:

Goal No. 3:
Why it aligns with my mission:

Goal No. 4:
Why it aligns with my mission:

Goal No. 5:
Why it aligns with my mission:

2. Is it really *our* goal?

This is a question that strikes many of us. Is the goal we have set out for ourselves purely a concoction of our own values and beliefs, a burning desire from inside our souls? Or is it something our "parents" mapped out for us? Is it a goal that peers pressure us to seek because they think we are good at it or will it only help them? Is it an objective that our families urge us to reach so they can forward *their* goals? Is it something that our country's leaders, our clergy members, or the people we respect suggest to us (for our own good, they say)? If our goals are not really *our* goals, there is a strong likelihood that we may question ourselves later and give up the chase after we exhaust a substantial amount of effort to reach them. Let's ensure that *our desires*, not the whims of others, drive our quests.

OPPORTUNITY:

List your major goals and write a sentence emphasizing why it is your goal and no one else's goal.

Goal No. 1:
Why it is my goal:

Goal No. 2:
Why it is my goal:

Goal No. 3:
Why it is my goal:

Goal No. 4:
Why it is my goal:

Goal No. 5:
Why it is my goal:

3. Is the goal precise?

Goals are not wishes. They are not bland preferences we may have. A goal that states, "I want to be a better person" is not very precise. A goal that states, "I will say hello to every person I meet and make them feel they are the most important person I talk to that day" is an explicit objective. A goal that proclaims, "I want to make more money" is vague and essentially powerless. A goal that reads, "I will add $10,000 to my income next year by turning my avocation into a second job" is more specific, and therefore, more effective. We must precisely state our goal. Turn "I want a new house" into "I will buy a new split-level ranch with a two-car garage, fireplace, and Jacuzzi in thirty-six months." Those who know exactly what they want have a much better chance in getting it.

We have met a young person like this one. Let's call him Johnny. Johnny brags at age twelve that "I want to be a writer, a doctor, or a lawyer when I grow up." Certainly these are lofty professions that Johnny heard his parents and friends say were jobs that could make him rich. Then, years later we find out Johnny is packing boxes at the Shop Quick grocery store as an adult. On the other hand, Johnny's classmate Jimmy who once said, "I want to be a jet test pilot in the Air Force, streaming through the skies flying the country's fastest planes!" Ten years later we find out that, doggone it, that's exactly what that kid is doing now. The difference between the two career goals is that Jimmy knew *exactly* what he wanted. Johnny outlined other professions that were not very specific or accurately in line with what *his* dream may have been. As a result, Johnny meandered through his young life, never forming a specific goal that would jump-start his brain into figuring out how he could reach his objective. I submit to you that the difference between Johnny and Jimmy lies less with the natural intelligence and educational opportunities they have, but more with the preciseness and vividness of the goals they set for themselves.

OPPORTUNITY:

Rewrite any of your goals that are not specific.

Goal No. 1:

Goal No. 2:

Goal No. 3:

Goal No. 4:

Goal No. 5:

4. Is our goal challenging, but achievable?

Management trainer Brian Tracy says goals should be "out of reach, but not out of sight."[45] That means our goals must be something that stretch our present ability to a new level. However, though we want to set exciting and grand goals for ourselves that may seem at first glance impossible to achieve, we must have a realistic and personal role in pursuing our goals. For example, a goal of "increasing my income by winning the $50 million dollar jackpot in this week's lotto game" is not very realistic, though it is precise.

There is a story of an old man named Harvey who desperately wanted to win the lotto daily number once in his life. He went to his place of worship and prayed to God, "Please Lord, once before I die, let me win the daily number." The next week nothing happened. Harvey went to worship again and prayed, "Please Lord, I am an old man and will die soon, please let me win the daily number." Again, no results. The third week Harvey knelt before the altar and prayed with all his might, "Lord, I promise I will not ask for another thing the rest of my life; just let me win the daily number once." Suddenly, there were streams of light from the top of the worship space and angelic singing echoing throughout the sanctuary. Harvey looked up at the light and heard a deep, echoing voice call, "Harvey!"

"Yes, Lord?" Harvey replied in awe.

"This is God," the booming heavenly voice said. "Meet me halfway, buy a ticket!"

Instead of acting like Harvey who expects to win without playing, we could set a goal that states, "I will invest $1,000 a year in stock, bond, and money market accounts to increase my savings for my children's education." That is a specific *and* challenging goal, especially if you never put away funds before. But, with effort and patience, it is achievable. Our goals should coax us out of our comfort zone in order for us to grow. An unrealistic goal sets us up for disappointment and discouragement. Small victories strung together make a powerful life, just as small wires wound together hold up tons on a suspension bridge. We should form goals as realistic as possible, but assure they are something that make us stretch to achieve.

OPPORTUNITY:

Write a short sentence how each of your major goals will stretch your ability.

Goal No. 1:

Goal No. 2:

Goal No. 3:

Goal No. 4:

Goal No. 5:

5. Does our goal emotionally excite us?

Why do some people sail through obstacles and reach their goals as easily as cruising on a magic flying carpet, while others give up before liftoff after they become frustrated, set back, or bored? The answer is *passion*. Passion and enthusiasm are the keys to maintaining our drive toward our objectives while we may be tempted to quit. Often, we hear of those who are at the top of their field in sports, medicine, or entertainment say that they have "always wanted to be" a professional sports player, a doctor, or an actor. Football quarterback great Dan Marino of the Miami Dolphins said while he was growing up in a depressed working-class neighborhood in Pittsburgh, he used to run through the streets dodging behind parked cars, throwing a football at telephone poles, pretending they were his receivers. In addition to his tremendous talent, he knew exactly what he wanted to accomplish and had a passion for achieving it. Anyone who follows professional sports is familiar with the "upsets" where a seemingly overmatched and inferior team defeats a superior squad of all-star players. How does this happen? The sports pundits usually say the lesser team "wanted to win more."

Talent and ranked position alone does not mean victory in the end. How many times have we heard someone say, "She has so much talent, but doesn't apply herself?" Talent must be combined with enthusiasm to create a focused vivacity to achieve new heights. In order for us to move consistently toward our goal, we must be more excited about achieving it than anything else. If we create a "passion" and supreme excitement, we will possess the required energy it takes to continue against any odds.

OPPORTUNITY:

Write a short sentence how each of your major goals emotionally excites you.

Goal No. 1:

Goal No. 2:

Goal No. 3:

Goal No. 4:

Goal No. 5:

6. Can we see ourselves accomplishing the goal?

Before many Olympic champion athletes have crossed the ribbon at the end of a race, hit the water after a perfect dive, or reached the finish line after a world-record downhill ski run, chances are it is not the first time they have been there in the winner's circle—even if they have never won a race before. Many champion athletes have been trained in the art of "visualization." Before these winners actually won, they already rehearsed it hundreds of times in their minds. NASA astronauts who strive to simulate the weightless environment they experience in space also use visualization. The concept is simple. Before we perform a task that we want to master, we "visualize" ourselves accomplishing that task in our mind before we attempt it.

We can draw a clear picture of what we desire with our mind's eye. Chances are we have already used this mental imagery. But we have not used visualization for our advantage, but rather we often use it against ourselves. Many times before we face a difficult assignment we "see" ourselves failing. More often than not, that is exactly what happens.

Instead of acting out the usual "negative" imagery to defeat our plans, let's use "positive" imagery to help us succeed.

We can call this imagery up at any time as we mentally rehearse our upcoming success. Jesus told his disciples, "When you pray, act as if your prayers have already been answered." If we pursue our goals with an attitude of distrust and fear, our minds will look for ways to sabotage our efforts. Many medical doctors tell us that the human brain cannot detect between real and imagined fears. If we see ourselves failing, we will most likely not be successful. Conversely, if we see ourselves succeeding, our minds will make every effort to make that rehearsed image come to reality. As we practice and pursue reaching our objectives, we need to act as if we already have attained mastery of our goal.

OPPORTUNITY:

For the next couple of minutes, fanaticize in your mind by visualizing yourself achieving your goal. Keep that memory fresh and repeat this often.

Finally, another famous Yogi Berra attribution: "Ninety percent of the game of baseball is mental," Berra supposedly claimed, "the other half is physical." Goal achievers also give more than 100 percent of their physical capabilities. They do it by using their "mind power" to visualize success before they ever achieve it in reality.

Have our stated goals held up to the Goal Litmus Test? If so, it is time to proceed to the *Six-Step Goal-Setting Action Plan.*

9

The Six-Step Goal-Setting Action Plan

Opportunity knocks but once.—William Shakespeare
Invite opportunity over and leave the door open!—David Waples

There are six simple steps to assemble your goal plan. However, though they are simple, all of the steps are important. (*Note a Six-Step Goal-Setting Action Plan boilerplate outline is at the back of this volume.*)

1. Write and See Our Goal Clearly

If you should put even a little on a little, and should do this often, soon this too would become big.—Hesiod

As mentioned previously, the conventional thinking in the goal-setting process maintains that goals must be written. Still, there are many top achievers who have never written a goal down on paper in their life. There goes that theory! But those goal achievers who have never spelled out their goal on paper actually have written their goal—they have etched it deeply in their minds.

We can take advantage of both schools of thought! First, yes we should put our pen to paper and write a clear, precise, challenging, but achievable goal. But we cannot stop there. We know what happens to those goals we make at the office during our annual assessment with the boss! Right! In the desk drawer they go, until we dust them off a week before our next review and come up with excuses why we have not achieved our goals! Whether written on paper or engraved into our minds, we must see and think about them every day! Preferably, we should review them several times a day.

Remember that our mind is like a magnet. That is, our mind will attract what it thinks about. Remember Napoleon Hill's research? His results claimed that any idea, "through repetition of thought and a burning desire, is constantly taken in by the subconscious." If we repeatedly think about our goal, our brains will constantly be working on ways we can achieve it. Goal-achievers who do not write goals on paper still manage to consciously and consistently think about achieving their objectives on a daily basis.

How do we achieve that level of concentration? Easy. First—for most of us—we should write our precise goal clearly. Then, we should hang our list of goals where we are likely to see it a couple of times a day. My suggestion—in the bathroom! Most likely, we will be there several times during the day with little else to concentrate on except for the crossword puzzle! We can keep a short version of our goals in a purse, a wallet, and a daily planner—anywhere we are likely to see it. Just by reading our goals over and over, our subconscious and conscious minds will actively be working on solutions to problems, routes around obstacles, and new paths to pursue. We will be visualizing and rehearsing our future success.

2. Give Reasons "Why"

I keep six honest men
(They taught me all I knew);
Their names are What and Why and When
And How and Where and Who.—Rudyard Kipling

We have all had the experience of pursuing a task and someone asks us, "Why are you doing that?" And we respond, "Gee, I don't really know." I bet this happens at work once in a while! Why do we pursue our goals if we are not sure why we need to reach them? If we applied the *Goal Litmus Test* discussed in the previous chapter, hopefully we have avoided this before we embark on our journey. That test reveals whether our goals are aligned with our most important beliefs, values, and designated purpose.

Asking "why" we are pursuing our goals is an extremely effective method of determining whether we will have the drive and passion to pursue them to the end. Do we really want to achieve our goals because it will make us better people or do we simply want to "outdo" the Joneses next door? Psychologists term these two motivational approaches as a "mastery goal perspective," which we engage to become more knowledgeable and skillful, or a "performance goal perspective," to be superior in performance (i.e., to "beat the other guy"). Our goal motivation may be a combination of both. But most studies reveal that the "mastery goal perspective" leads to more beneficial outcomes.[46] In other words, we need to improve *our* prior performance.

First, like our beliefs, the continual drive to reach our goals is supported like legs hold up a table. We must have clear, strong reasons that are not only supported by basic unwavering principles, but also motivated by the positive march toward desired pleasure and the negative retreat from pain. This is remarkably effective when we are attempting to achieve a goal that is not easy for us. In fact, the discipline to reach the ultimate result may be somewhat painful.

I once was learning to speak Italian in preparation for a possible trip to Italy. I was eager and pursued my Italian lessons with a passion since I kept thinking of the challenge and enjoyment I would experience when I went on the journey. I would see a foreign country for the first time and have a wonderful experience. However, I later changed my mind and cancelled the trip. Since I had hours, days, weeks, and months dedicated to Italian lessons, I decided to continue with the instruction since I had invested so much time into it. But after a while, I became bored with the effort and more and more the language drills seemed like a fatiguing and laboring chore. I then realized I had lost my reasons "why" I was learning. Though I still had an interest, I dropped the lessons and devoted my time to achieve goals that I had real "whys" to achieve. We must carefully look at our activities and stated goals. Do we really have enough reasons "why" to keep us passionate in our hunt? If not, "Arrivederci!"

As I mentioned in a previous chapter, I used this method when I began an exercise program to lose weight and improve my level of health. To forward the discipline to continue my fitness program beyond my "good intentions," I outlined three reasons to achieve my goal: two positive value *benefits* (improved appearance and fun), and one *penalty* (sickness). Now I usually exercise several times a week. Hopefully, working to improve my physical condition will more likely lead to a longer, healthier, and consequently, happier life. There are no guarantees, but more important than the total years of my life, is the health and happiness I enjoy during the years that I have.

Because physical fitness is a lifestyle change and an ongoing and never-ending goal, we need to keep these motivational power pills fresh in our minds every day. For example, I habitually look at my watch at about 11:27 a.m. every day of the workweek. That is because I work out during my lunch hour. Ultimately, this is a mind-relaxing and physical stimulant for me in the middle of the day. When I used to leave the office chair for a lunch counter stool at a restaurant I would often eat too large of a meal. As a result, I would be sluggish the rest of the day. Instead, the mid-day exercise break invigorates me. I eat less and remain more alert and active in the afternoon than many others who simply "go out to lunch."

However, you may get the impression that I leap out of my office chair and race to the local YMCA with a broad smile, impatiently waiting to jump on the Stairmaster. Do you want to know how many times I feel motivated to go the YMCA and exercise during the week? Five times? Three times? Two times? How about ZERO! That's right, I *never* feel like leaving my warm office to trudge through the snow or rain to punish my body and work up a sweat. Using our "whys" to endure temporary discomfort in breaking through to our goal is the additional power we receive when we exercise our discipline. Because it is a *habit* motivated by the positive and negative values of moving toward ultimate pleasure and fleeing from undesired consequences, my exercise routine is rarely broken. In addition, though I never *want* to go to the health club, ten minutes after I arrive and begin exercising, the pleasure of the aerobic activity makes me happy I made the decision! When I am finished, I cannot imagine why I ever hesitated to go in the first place. Until the next day at 11:27 a.m.!

The saying, "Habits are made, not born" is true. It is said that we make our habits and then our habits make us. Building good habits takes not only consistent effort, but also good solid reasons why that habit is right for us. Whether our goal is to enforce our good habits by exercising, staying on a healthy low-fat diet, making that extra phone call to reach another client, or spending extra time with our family or in our intimate relationships, the power of "whys" should come into place. By taking that first step, we can build a sometimes difficult and tedious task into a routine habit and not fall back into lethargic, unproductive practices. As a result, we will find additional "gold" at the end of our goal rainbow.

OPPORTUNITY:

For each of your top goals, list at least three benefits if you achieve your goal and consequences if you don't. List why you want to accomplish them. A goal without reasons why is like a table without legs. Without them, you'll end up flat on the floor!

Goal No. 1:

Positive "whys"

-

-

-

Negative "whys"

-

-

-

Goal No. 2:

Positive "whys"

-

-

-

Negative "whys"

-

-

-

Goal No. 3:

Positive "whys"

-
-
-

Negative "whys"

-
-
-

Goal No. 4:

Positive "whys"

-
-
-

Negative "whys"

-
-
-

Goal No. 5:

Positive "whys"

-

-

-

Negative "whys"

-

-

-

3. List Any Challenges We Must Face

Man's mind once stretched by a new idea, never regains its original dimension.—Oliver Wendell Holmes

It is foolhardy and "Pollyanna" to whistle in the dark while journeying toward our goals without anticipating any bumps in the night. We face obstacles as we venture up our mountainous expedition. Some obstacles are obvious and some are hidden. Though we need to take heed of these stumbling blocks, we should not turn the hurdles into insurmountable barriers that prevent us from keeping in motion.

Our obstacles or problems we face are actually "opportunities" in disguise. The reason these impediments are before us is to teach us the proper lessons necessary before we elevate ourselves to the next step in our goal trek. We can either be defeated by these lessons by adopting the attitude of, "See, I told you it wouldn't work," or we can accept each challenge we confront as a lesson by saying, "This effort has yielded an unsuccessful result, what else can I try?"

We have a plethora of natural obstacles we confront when pursuing our goal journey. It may be our age, our limited experience, discrimination in the workplace, lack of an educational degree, physical handicaps, unsupportive families, poor financial health, etc. All of these obstacles are only conditions that can be modified, overcome, or ignored. For example, here are three examples of overcoming obstacles:

- The business failure of his haberdashery did not discourage young Harry in pursuing another career. Harry used his business experience as a lesson that one can recover from failure. Harry pursued a career in local politics that led to the U.S. Senate. "Harry" Truman also became president of the United States.

- The physical handicap of having a deformed right arm did not stop "Jim" from playing baseball. Jim would pitch with his left arm and then toss his glove from his shortened right arm onto his left to field the ball hit back to him. "Jim" Abbott eventually became a major league baseball pitching star.

- As an African-American, young "Colin" faced racial discrimination throughout his life. While mopping floors in a Pepsi-Cola bottling plant, he did not stop working hard to show he was smart enough to run the bottling machines they only let "whites" operate. Colin then began a career in the Army. "Colin" Powell eventually became the Chairman of the Joint Chiefs of Staff directing the United States' effort in winning the Gulf War, and later was named U.S. Secretary of State.

One thing in common among nearly all successful people is the realization that everyone faces obstacles, even if those blocks are only in their own mind. Before taking the field in the competitive game of life, we need to "know the opposition." That means identifying our weak points. We must make a list of obstacles we may face on our journey. If we write down the potential roadblocks, our minds can work on detours around them.

"God does not give us burdens we cannot carry." That familiar maxim we are likely to hear from a rabbi, minister, or priest may be difficult to swallow in light of many of life's tragedies. Sometimes we *do* need help in lifting the burdens life drops on us. With or without help, facing obstacles and breaking through barriers tends to increase our capability to withstand the strong and bitter winds of life's disappointments and proves that we can endure. German-Swiss philosopher and writer Friedrich Nietzsche said, "He who has a why to live for can bear with almost any how," and "That which does not kill me, makes me stronger." Like lifting weights at the gym, our obstacle-handling muscles will get stronger as we practice climbing over them.

We all have an expanding *sphere of capability*. Imagine a three-dimensional sphere that is a metaphor representing our ability to contend with life's circumstances. There are circumstances—small problems that we have experienced—within this sphere that we have learned to manage. As an infant, our sphere of capability is quite small, and we depend on our parents to protect us. As we grow through our childhood and adolescence, our sphere becomes larger. Our ability to manage problems naturally grows with it. But there are always larger obstacles and problems in our life that exist just outside this area that we believe we cannot handle. Once we reach adulthood, however, we may not be forced to continue to expand our sphere of capability to handle new problems. We may stay in our "shell" and refuse to deal with or even acknowledge challenges that are right outside our area of influence. However, if we take the challenge and reach out and encounter the obstacle, our sphere—our problem-solving ability—expands geometrically in all directions. As a result, we can deal with even unrelated impediments we previously may have lacked the courage to confront.

There is always an example of a nearly insurmountable burden individuals bear. It is a hardship so great or an event so tragic, we wonder how anyone could ever recover. It is said that only at the bottom of the deepest, darkest well, can we see the dimmest star in the black sky above. That may explain how many people who were dealt a tough hand by life's deal landed at the bottom of the well and later recovered to soar to great heights, chasing loftier goals than ever before. We see these rags-to-riches stories and wonder what caused the turnaround. And it is not only in the movies where Indiana Jones escapes virtual death to rescue the beautiful damsel and snatch the treasure at the climax of the movie. It happens in real life.

OPPORTUNITY:

When you face tough obstacles in your path, you must know them, understand them, but don't lose sight of your goals. Your mind has the power to compose alternatives when all seems to be lost. For each of your major goals, make a list of potential obstacles and what you can do to maneuver around them.

Goal No. 1:

Obstacles

-
-
-

Goal No. 2:

Obstacles

-
-
-

Goal No. 3:

Obstacles

-
-
-

Goal No. 4:

Obstacles

-
-
-

Goal No. 5:

Obstacles

-
-
-

4. Find Out Who Can Help Us

Each friend represents a world in us, a world possibly not born until they arrive, and it is only by this meeting that a new world is born.—Anaïs Nin

A memory that always brings a tear to my eye is seeing comedian Jerry Lewis thirty years ago at the end of his Labor Day Telethon benefiting the fight against Muscular Dystrophy. Exhausted after pulling the twenty-four-hour TV stint, he sang "You'll Never Walk Alone" to a child with the dreadful disease. Though these children face tremendous obstacles, those that love them will make sure they will have help. When we carve out ambitious goals for ourselves, we may feel over-matched by the tremendous task in front of us. But remember, with effective goal-setting, we do not have to "walk alone."

We should make a list of people that can help us work toward our goals. They may be friends, relatives, colleagues, supervisors, or subordinates. Most likely, if we have a goal in mind, someone else has already achieved it. Why reinvent the wheel? Let's contact these people and ask them how they did it! Those individuals who have reached great accomplishments are proud of their achievements and are usually very unselfish in sharing their "secrets" of success. People love to talk about themselves and their accomplishments. Let's take advantage of that personality trait and absorb as much information as we can.

Many times we can create a mentor-protégé relationship if we are attempting to reach new heights. Mentors often find helping others assist in maintaining their own motivation for creating new goals for themselves. Protégés can benefit from the experience and knowledge of another person without spending thousands of dollars at an expensive university. I admire teachers of all kinds. But we have heard the unfortunate epigram: "Those who can, do; those who can't, teach." For some that may be true, but for most, I do not subscribe to that premise. Those who have "been there and done that" can be incredible teachers simply by talking about their efforts. It is easy to pick out the pedants from the professors by seeking those with dirty fingernails from accomplishing significant feats. Not only can these people be good instructors, but they also can be a reservoir of inspiration for us to refill our motivational fuel tank when we feel it is getting low.

Modeling is an essential technique of goal achieving. Modeling is not copying or stealing. All great heroes and heroines can point to champions they revered. This admiration of models is not a sycophantic idolization. They are symbols of respect and encouragement. If we seek to be great in our field of endeavor, it stands to reason that we should acquire as much knowledge as those who already excelled in the same calling. Even Thomas Jefferson, primary author of the Declaration of

Independence, read and was inspired by the great works of Locke and other political philosophers. They not only gave him the ideas of life, liberty, and the pursuit of happiness, but also acted as a great stimulus for the courage to declare Colonial America's independence.

Most noteworthy performers have perhaps lesser-known, but immensely important, instructors who nourished their growth. Plato had the oral lessons of Socrates. All great musical virtuosos in an orchestra benefit from a conductor to help direct their way. Standing behind great actors are great directors and behind Olympic champions are inspiring trainers. Modeling for inspiration is apparent today in the world of sports. Basketball superstar and international icon Michael Jordan revered the African-American baseball pioneer Jackie Robinson. On the sideline directing sports legends are great coaches that assist their players' development and bring out the best in them. Football Hall of Fame running back Gale Sayers admitted that Chicago Bears' coach "Papa Bear" George Halas played a critical role in developing his talent. Today's young golfers model footsteps in the fairway of those who came before them. Few professionals on the tour today would deny that they were influenced by the careers of Jack Nicholas, Ben Hogan, or master teachers such as the great golf instructor Harvey Pennick. Even Ken Griffey Jr., one of baseball's greatest contemporary hitters, sought the advice of hitting-legend Ted Williams in order to improve his swing.

One note of caution, however. We must seek assistance from people who have our best interests at heart, or at least, do not oppose us in achieving our goals. We may have fair-weather friends, jealous family members, envious work associates, or other powerful detractors that would like nothing more than to see us fail. Even those closest to us can act like sand in the greased wheels of success. They may not wish to consciously see us hurt, but their own lack of ambition and frustration may cause them to naysay and rain on our parade. Author and motivational speaker Les Brown has a term for these folks: *toxic people*. Brown says there are two kinds of people that we come into contact with: those who nourish us and cheer from the sidelines as we race toward the finish line of our goals; and toxic people who poison us with their pessimism. Brown suggests avoiding those toxic people and seek only nourishment from those who want to see us grow in our lives.[47] We need as much encouragement as possible to pursue our goals with passion. If we find that no one around us can provide this guidance and words of support, let's not declare our goals publicly. We can keep our goals to ourselves and act *as if* our closest friends are our most ardent supporters. They will never know the help they give us.

When my wife, Barbara, was competing in the 100th anniversary running of the Boston Marathon, more than a million people lined the streets heading into downtown Boston to cheer on the more than 40,000 runners participating in the historic race. She strained a ligament in the tenth mile of the twenty-six-mile journey and found it very painful to continue. All along the racecourse, people held up signs supporting their family members or friends. "Go Jim!" and "Run, Mom, Run!" the signs stated. To battle the pain and motivate her to complete the race, Barbara used her imagination and pretended that *every* sign read "Go Barb!" and "Run, Barb, Run!" This fantasy cheering section helped her find the strength to complete the race, despite the incredible discomfort.

We can develop our own models, and coaches, whether they consciously help us or not. Let's form, or perhaps "imagine," our own cheering fans to make sure we are playing to win our goals in front of the home team crowd!

OPPORTUNITY:

List those models, teachers, and allies who can help you toward your goal by their knowledge, example, or support, and write why they motivate you.

Goal No. 1:

Models, teachers, coaches, allies

-
-
-

Goal No. 2:

Models, teachers, coaches, allies

-
-
-

Goal No. 3:

Models, teachers, coaches, allies

-
-
-

Goal No. 4:

Models, teachers, coaches, allies

-
-
-

Goal No. 5:

Models, teachers, coaches, allies

-
-
-

5. What Skills and Knowledge are Necessary?

Knowledge is Power.—Francis Bacon

I have mentioned repeatedly throughout this book that just about anyone can accomplish just about anything. However, despite the ambition, motivation, and determination we possess in our secret stockpile of goal weapons, we cannot achieve our objectives unless we know what must be done. Unless we acquire the skills and knowledge necessary to achieve our goals, well-intentioned efforts may prove fruitless. That does not mean that we must be experts when we are beginning our goal-setting quest, nor do we have to hold an encyclopedia of information in our heads, either. But, we must know what we need to know to realize a positive result from our efforts.

Surveys show that only *one out of every twenty* adults ever reads a non-fiction book (other than the personal lives of Hollywood celebrities) or listens to an instructional tape after their formal education ends. I find that figure nearly inconceivable and astounding! That's only five percent! Coincidentally, that is about the same percentage of people who have some type of written goals for themselves! Any surprise?

One reason many people may not seek out the knowledge they must obtain to achieve their "dreams" may be a *lack of confidence.* "Learning is for the young," they say. However, an increasing number of older adults now enter higher-educational institutions and senior citizens take computer classes to prepare for life in the new century. The absorption of knowledge does not magically stop when we take our last final in high school or turn in our last term paper in college. As you probably heard at our high school or college graduation, "Your learning is just beginning."

We are probably familiar with Ben Franklin's epigram: "An investment in knowledge pays the greatest interest." Most of us are extremely concerned with money in our bank account. Why are we less concerned with the growth of wealth in our knowledge account? Okay, okay, we know we need the right data in today's "information age" to achieve our goals. But we are no Ben Franklin or Albert Einstein, we modesty claim. Where do we start?

When is the last time we visited the public library? Sure, we take the kids every once in a while, but do we actively search the shelves for the knowledge that will act as necessary fuel to propel ourselves out of an atmosphere of stagnation? As stated before, someone else has accomplished most of our personal or professional goals at a previous time, and chances are, someone wrote about it. Our libraries contain all the knowledge in the world. At our fingertips is all the information, motivation, strategy, and tips we would ever want to download into our minds. And here is the kicker! It is free! Or I should say we are already paying for it through our city, county, state, and federal taxes. So let's use it! If we want to increase our physical muscles, we must exercise them. If we want to augment our mind power to navigate the treacherous waters in search of our "New World" of goals, we must discipline our mind.

Knowledge *is* power. Those people with expertise, skills, and information that others do not have are highly sought after. We can increase our power by finding the information we need or, at least, know where to find it when we need it. Browsing our local library on a regular basis will stimulate our mind as it never was aroused before. Skimming through the recent releases and grazing through the classics will make us feel like a kid in a candy store with a pocketful of nickels.

"Hey, wait a minute," you say. Sure the library is chock full of information, but "I've got a busy life. I have to pick up the kids at soccer practice, make dinner, call my mother, attend the PTA, and stay late at the office. I don't have time to read! And, besides, when I get around to it, I'll surf the World Wide Web!"

For those of us still making excuses of why we do not gather new knowledge and information, the audiotape/CD erases that defense. We can find thousands of books and other publications on audiotapes/CDs both abridged and unabridged. Imagine what it takes to listen to an audiotape/CD. It takes, well, not much. You just have to sit there. Like a bump on a log, right? We know how to do that. Some of us are pretty good at it. Still many of us do not have time to sit around. So, don't.

We can turn our car into what motivation experts call "automobile university." If we set a stopwatch on the amount of time we spend in our car during a week, riding the bus, train, or subway, we would be astonished. Federal data released in January 2003, stated that Americans increased their driving 11 percent since 1995.[48] Though our most important task in driving a car is the safe control of the vehicle, unlike cell phones, listening to audio books can be conducted without impairing our ability to drive. A 2001 study by the National Safety Council found that cell phone conversations create much higher levels of driver distractions than listening to the radio or audio books.[49] We have grown up listening to the car radio—perhaps it is now time to absorb valuable information through our ears instead of the same old ditty and car-dealer commercial for the hundredth time. Do you think you can absorb some knowledge while you do the dishes, clean the house, wash the laundry, rake the leaves, cut the grass, go for a walk, take a bath, get dressed in the morning, lay on the beach, etc., etc., etc? Is it really that difficult? We need to go to the public library today, borrow some audiotapes/CDs and plug in! We will be entertained, informed, provoked, and energized. We can learn a new language, brush up on history, improve goal-setting techniques, or become thoroughly schooled in our chosen career field. All it takes is a pair of ears! Or even just one.

Another way to acquire the skills and knowledge we need in the midst of a busy lifestyle is to turn our down time into "up" time. This is accomplished by reading magazines, articles, books, and other material available when we are sitting in the doctor's office, waiting to pick up the kids from their numerous extra-circular activities, traveling by bus or plane, taking a break, or eating lunch at work. Wherever we are, we can have some type of information about our goals with us. It helps keep our goals fresh in our brain and stimulates our conscious mind in motivating ourselves to continue the pursuit of our purpose.

But how do we know what information to get? There are millions of books in thousands of categories and no time to cover it all. As we did with our goal planning, we need to make another list. First, let's start on the positives. We need to jot down strengths in skills and knowledge we already have. We must recognize what we already know, and then identify our aptitude in various subjects. Once we know our strong points, it is easy to distinguish what areas of skills and knowledge we need to improve. By comparing these areas with the requirements to achieve our goal, we will know what we must work on.

It is also wise to use audiotapes/CDs and books that are biographical in nature. By reading and listening to the life stories of notable men and women throughout history, we generate motivation necessary to move us toward our destination. When we hear the life journeys of these celebrated individuals, we discover more often than not that they are not necessarily *extraordinary* people. They are *ordinary* people who have done *extraordinary* things. We are no different. We are also ordinary people. But we are capable of extraordinary accomplishments by pursuing our dreams.

Do not stop the process of self-learning. It must be continual improvement. Those that stand still get left behind. Let's attend that adult education class we always wanted to take. Let's complete that degree that eluded us for so long. In this world, we will not get another chance. Life is not a dress rehearsal. This is the *show*. We must live it now! Learn from the experts. Get the skills of a professional by learning from one. Never give up on the pursuit of knowledge because it will never fail us when we attempt to grasp it.

The search for enlightenment and wisdom is a lifelong journey and it is not accomplished by drinking a magic potion that will elucidate us. It is a continual and never-ending tour of truth and self-improvement. Remember the Chinese proverb: "The best time to plant a tree was twenty years ago. The second best time is right now!" By living these words, we already are on the journey.

OPPORTUNITY:

List the various kinds of resources that can help you toward your goals. They can include classes, books, tapes, magazines, Internet web sites, seminars, lectures, etc.

Goal No. 1:

Resources

-
-
-

Goal No. 2:

Resources

-
-
-

Goal No. 3:

Resources

-
-
-

Goal No. 4

Resources

-
-
-

Goal No. 5:

Resources

-
-
-

6. Plan of Immediate Action with a Victory Date

The test of any man lies in action.—Pindar

We have written our goals, stated why we want to achieve them, noted any challenges or obstacles we may face, identified who can help us get there, and inventoried any potential skills and knowledge we need to obtain. Now what? Well, we must plan our work and then work our plan. We must chart a course of action. Most important, if we want the momentum of goal-setting to get rolling, we must take *immediate* action. The action does not have to be grandiose or profound, it can be simple and completed without much effort. But it needs to be done now!

Once we have completed the previous five steps, we need to take some kind of action *today* that demonstrates to our mind that we are very serious about pursuing this goal. We cannot let one day go by before we take this action. If we do, the chance of success declines dramatically. We can lose our edge. As the maxim says, "Strike while the iron is hot." If our goal is to lose weight, we must do something today that forms a commitment:

- We could call a health club and give them our credit card number (a financial commitment); or

- Go into the kitchen and throw out all our fattening food into the garbage (an emotional commitment); or

- Take an extended walk to warm up your muscles for a daily schedule of exercise (a physical commitment).

By taking *immediate* action, we will either plunge or slowly dip our foot into uncertain waters. But the point is we will make a commitment that helps insure future action. Our brain will start working on ways to achieve our objectives. And our mind will begin to believe, "I can do this." This power of belief, commitment, and action will get us to where we want to go. And along with getting started, we need to plan when we plan to finish.

A word about "deadlines." I mentioned earlier that we must have a deadline when we plan our goals. But "deadline" is a scary word. The only "deadline" we will surely reach is when we are pushing up daisies. A better term might be "victory date." By attaching victory dates to our goal plans, we install a target time to reach various steps toward our goals. Although in some cases it can be a motivating "negative" force, when we miss a "deadline," we may become upset, frustrated, or depressed. We might likely decide to dump our goal if we miss one or more "deadlines." If we do not reach our proposed "victory date," there is no need to worry. Simply "reschedule" the date on which we will claim "victory" of our accomplishment. We would all rather plan a party than a funeral, so let's do it!

Here is a personal story that demonstrates the goal-setting process. When I began dating the wonderful woman I would one day marry, I came to see her compete in a triathlon. This athletic competition involved more than a one-half-mile swim in open water, a twenty-three-mile bike ride over rolling country hills, and a six-mile uphill and downhill run, one event after another. Watching the competition, I was amazed at the participants. I admired anyone who would dare attempt, let alone finish, such an event. I dreamed (but not too seriously) that someday I could do the same thing. During the following months I continued to think about competing in the event the following year but later rejected it citing that it would take too much training and I lacked the "fire in the belly" to pursue it.

Eleven months later and only four weeks before the next event, I was offered a free entry to compete in the race. My fiancée was injured from the Boston Marathon experience and was advised by her doctor not to race. The free entry offer was made at a wedding reception, and after a dose of "liquid courage," I vowed that I would compete in my fiancée's stead.

"Can I train for this event in a month?" I asked my fiancée.

"*I* can't train for the event in a month!" said Barbara, a veteran marathon runner.

"That's where I'll prove you wrong!" I said, wisely giving her the car keys.

Within three seconds of waking the next morning, reality hit me like a cast-iron frying pan in the face. Compete in a triathlon! In four weeks! And I never ran more than two miles in my life. I don't even like to run! Then I remembered the challenge I agreed to, accepted it, and initiated the goal-setting process. I rose from bed and began:

1. *I wrote down my goal:* "I will compete in and finish the triathlon four weeks from today."

2. *I gave myself three reasons why:* "I accepted a challenge and my pride was on the line. I did dream of competing in the event to experience the thrill of completing such an accomplishment. And I was going to run for my fiancée, who could not compete due to injury (ah, love, what a great motivator!).

3. *I listed my challenges and obstacles*: Time! Endurance! Breath! Pain!

4. *I jotted down who could help me:* my fiancée could not run, but she could coach. I took her advice, benefiting from a champion who had done it before. She served both as a model and cheering section.

5. *I recorded the skills and knowledge necessary.* I read running, biking, health, and swimming magazines, and recorded what I needed on race day and what equipment I needed to rent or purchase.

6. *I wrote down in my planner an immediate action strategy.* I composed a plan for each of the twenty-eight days I had to train. I then immediately put on my sneakers before I could change my mind and started running that morning in the rain.

It was an intimidating, grueling process for me. What other athletic types did on a routine basis was an incredible challenge in my book. But everyday as I swam, biked, or ran, I kept the vision of myself crossing the finish line, ecstatic at my personal accomplishment. Four weeks later, with my coach and rooting section beside me, I finished 262nd out of 282 competitors in the triathlon. Not impressive by race standards, but I finished, which, by the way, was my goal. The delight and satisfaction I felt when I sprinted (ha!) across the finish line was unlike anything I had ever experienced in my life. And, it could not have been done without the *Six-Step Goal-Setting Action Plan*. But how do we best make the first step? We need to understand how the *Goal Motivation Wheel* rolls.

10

Let's Roll—The Goal Motivation Wheel

One must learn by doing the thing; for though you think you know it, you have no certainty until you try.—Sophocles

Have you ever wondered which came first, the chicken or the egg? While that enduring enigma ponders philosophers and biologists, we can apply that riddle to another puzzle. Which comes first:

- *conviction,*
- *motivation,*
- *activity,* or
- *results?*

These four steps are on the circumference of what I call the *Goal Motivational Wheel.* The wheel—just a simple disk that spins in a journey from one location to another—is said to be early man's great invention. But how does the *Goal Motivational Wheel* start spinning? Can we jump on the perimeter anywhere and go along for the ride? That's easy when the disc is already in motion, but what is the easiest way to start our "goal ball" rolling in the first place?

Imagine we are standing behind a heavy, seemingly immovable, wheel on a flat surface that we must start moving forward. We can try to start to rotate the *Goal Motivation Wheel* by bending down at the base of our wheel and push upward with *conviction*. I mentioned earlier that ultimate goal achievement is not possible without a firm conviction, or belief, that we can actually reach our objective. But where is conviction in the goal cycle? It is on the bottom heading upwards. To form a conviction mighty enough to push this mass upward, we would need strong beliefs, which are easier after achieving proven, persuasive results. If we are trying to get a substantial goal in motion, it is possible to get movement, but it is a struggle. There is an easier way. But, don't give up, let's examine the next possibility, *motivation*.

Motivation is certainly an essential part of a successful revolution of our goal wheel, and it certainly helps to possess a conviction that goal attainment is possible if we are to be motivated to achieve. But again, where is motivation on the circumference of the wheel? On the top of the wheel in front of us, motivation is much higher than conviction and seemingly a logical place to start pushing. But still we face a bit of a challenging shove before we get "over the hump" and head forward. What happens if we have little motivation that we will be successful? Can we still turn the wheel? It is possible, but there is even an easier way to get started.

For the moment, let's skip over *activity*, which resides on the front side of the wheel away from us. At the bottom of the other side of the wheel that first hits the road as we would propel forward is *results*. This is a real chicken-and-egg problem. How can we get results unless we do something to move toward our goal? And we cannot get any results unless we have had some activity—action conducted by the goal-makers, (i.e., us).

Since logically we cannot begin at results, let's return to *activity*. Here is an area of our goal wheel that can actually cause definite motion once we push on it. Activity is placed where we are now moving downward on the wheel. Assuming we are in a position of normal gravity, we can let the natural power of the earth's force work to move us downward and start the goal wheel moving. In other words, if we want to get immediate results toward our goal, we must get active, and do something—*anything*—first, whether we feel committed or motivated or not!

"But wait a minute," all us couch potatoes exclaim. Here lies the crux of the puzzle that often eludes us. *We cannot get results unless we take action.* Unless we have some tangible evidence, it is difficult to come up with the belief that we can actually achieve more results. However, with actual results, we increase our conviction and that can create additional motivation. Once our motivation to accomplish a goal is augmented, we will then commit to more activity that will be much easier the second time around. We know the first step is always the toughest. With expanded action on our part, we in turn produce more results. With each subsequent action, the revolutions of our wheel turn faster and our overall velocity toward our goal accelerates. Before we know it, we are "cruising" toward our goals.

But how do we take action if we are not motivated? How do we get motivated if we have no conviction? This is where we have to stretch. This is where we have to reach down inside of ourselves and engage our "auxiliary" power to thrust us through enemy territory. Remember the force of gravity. Sometimes all we have to do is "take the plunge" and life's gravity takes over. We must take action, but not as much as we may think.

Here is an example. This first time I took my children sledding on the "big hill" at a nearby park, their eyes became as wide as the saucer sleds in their hands when they saw the grade of the hill I wanted them to slide down. "We're not going down that, Daddy!" they shivered.

"Don't worry," I assured them, trying to assuage their fears. "This is nothing, you'll love it!"

They were not so sure. Getting to the top of the hill, I pledged to them that I would hold their sleds at the top until they got used to it, and if they did not want to go down, they did not have to. I lied.

Bad Daddy!

Once they were at the top of the hill, I said, "OOPS's!" and let go the sled. Their voices echoed as they accelerated down the hill, "Noooooooooo!"

Mean Daddy! Cruel Daddy!

As I watched them barrel down the snowy hill shouting, "Hang on!" I said a silent prayer and pleaded that they would not fall off and get a bloody nose. Fortunately they incurred no injury, at least that time. But would you guess what they said when I slid down to meet them? I expected, "Daddy, you lied to us! Mean Daddy! Cruel Daddy!" I was ready for the wrath. But instead, they said, "Let's do it again, Dad!"

Whether we are sledding down a hill, diving off a diving board, or facing a long-term fear that plopped a road block in front of our goal, sometimes we must get "pushed" to get a result. Once we take a plunge, we can identify some nugget of positive product out of the result that will create a conviction—a belief that yes, we can do it! Once we get one revolution of the motivation wheel, we find it rolls smoother as we go along. And we will need momentum when we reach bumps in the road and uphill challenges in the future. Great invention, that wheel!

Take action first! Let's worry about our conviction and motivation later. First, we must take action, and then the next time around will be smoother, faster, and easier. If a large action is too intimidating, make a small, less-ostentatious step. If our goal is to keep our house clean on a regular basis, we should not try to mop the floor, wash the dishes, scrub the walls, and vacuum all in one fell swoop. Take a small action. Just wash a dish! When we see the results—that sparkly dish with our smiling face reflecting on it—we will be so satisfied we will probably wash another one. After a few rotations on the wheel, watch out, we will be cleaning our little hearts out. We need to pick a small action to take toward one of our goals. Do it immediately and see what is produced. But, by all means, just do it!

Eating an Elephant—Break Goals Down Into Smaller Steps

...I have promises to keep, and miles to go before I sleep.—Robert Frost

How do you eat an elephant? Well, of course, one bite at a time. Don't expect to conquer the world in a day. When I was young, I had a very large dog, a German Shepherd-Collie mix named Max. Max could swallow an entire hot dog with a single gulp. However, if we tried to do the same thing, we would choke to death. That is why we must break our goals down into edible chunks that we can chew and digest. In the 1960s television comedy-drama series *Room 222*, actress Karen Valentine portrayed a rookie teacher in a tough high school. At the end of her first rocky and tumultuous day, she reviewed her mistakes, trials, and tribulations with her colleagues. A veteran teacher instructed her, "Don't expect to become a perfect teacher in a day." "Oh, of course not," her perky character answered, "I'm going to give it a week." We can be positive, but not careless, or we may choke. Therefore, we need to break our goals down in specific steps and we must attach a date of accomplishment to the rungs of our goal ladder.

In order to be successful goal-setters, we need to integrate our long-term objectives with our daily activities. That is not always easy. We cannot set long-term goals, but not take action on a daily basis. If we do take daily action, we will likely be happier. But start small. College basketball coach Rick Pitino writes in his book *Success is a Choice* that striving toward short-term goals is a strength-building exercise that leads to a positive work ethic that in the long run, breeds larger successes.[50] A study published in the *Journal of Personality* revealed that progress at daily goals relevant to accomplishing one's life goals was significantly more strongly related to "subjective well-being" [happiness] than progress at daily goals that were *unrelated* to one's life goals. The authors of the study state "...some daily goals may be building blocks toward an imagined future or escape routes from a dreaded life outcome."[51] This is the pleasure-pain principle once again. Either way, slow and steady wins the race, but we have miles to go before we sleep.

Review Goals and Monitor Progress Daily

If you can't measure it, you can't manage it.—Anonymous

If we spend hours defining our mission, categorizing our values, brainstorming our goals, and analyzing our strategy, the last thing we should do is to write our plans on paper and file them away in a filing cabinet, in a box of personal items in the attic lost among canceled checks, or stuffed in a drawer. As our grandmothers taught us, out of sight, out of mind. Our goals must be in front of us on a daily basis to be effective.

Most important, we must monitor our progress on a regular basis. After we have filled out our goal planner, we need another page to track our progress. By reviewing if we are keeping to our planned schedule, we can physically see how we are doing with our plan. This tracking sheet will encourage us as we make progress. Even with a positive attitude and good intentions, we can become lackluster if we do not see actual progress in our journey. By jotting down where we are in the course of our goal track, we will receive satisfaction, conviction, and motivation when we observe motion!

OPPORTUNITY:

First, you need to select immediate actions to take on your overall goal. Estimate the amount of time it will take for each step on the way to your destination. If your goal is a long-term one, split the effort into three categories—Immediate, Intermediate, and Long-Term. Also, list daily activities that will propel you toward your goal.

Goal No. 1:

A. *Immediate Objectives*: Up to one month   Completion date

B. *Intermediate Objectives*: One to Six Months   Completion date

C. *Long-range Objectives*: Six months to three years   Completion date

D. *Daily activities* that help you to reach your goal

Goal No. 2:

A. *Immediate Objectives*: Up to one month   Completion date

B. *Intermediate Objectives*: One to Six Months   Completion date

C. *Long-range Objectives*: Six months to three years   Completion date

D. *Daily activities* that help you to reach your goal

Goal No. 3:

A. *Immediate Objectives*: Up to one month   Completion date

B. *Intermediate Objectives*: One to Six Months   Completion date

C. *Long-range Objectives*: Six months to three years   Completion date

D. *Daily activities* that help you to reach your goal

Goal No. 4

A. *Immediate Objectives*: Up to one month   Completion date

B. *Intermediate Objectives*: One to Six Months   Completion date

C. *Long-range Objectives*: Six months to three years   Completion date

D. *Daily activities* that help you to reach your goal

Goal No. 5:

A. *Immediate Objectives*: Up to one month   Completion date

B. *Intermediate Objectives*: One to Six Months   Completion date

C. *Long-range Objectives*: Six months to three years   Completion date

D. *Daily activities* that help you to reach your goal

By splitting our goals into immediate, intermediate, and long-range objectives, we will not choke on the task before us. But once we break our goals down, outlining completion of the next step is not as "Polly-anna" as proposing to accomplish the entire goal in an unrealistic time frame. While we should visualize crossing the finish line of our goal to help motivate us to action, our major focus should be the next rung on the ladder. We cannot climb upward unless we securely step on each rung. There is no need to look too far ahead—we have already made our plan.

Remember that Chinese proverb mentioned earlier: "The longest journey begins with a single step." We have discussed the first step is usually the most difficult to take. But once we move forward with the *Goal Motivation Wheel,* we are on our way to our ultimate destination. As we progress, we also need to adopt *Goal DOERS' Winning Qualities.*

11

Goal DOERS' Winning Qualities

The secret of success is constancy to purpose.—Benjamin Disraeli

The secret of success is not so secret. Those champion goal-achievers, whether they are celebrated in the media, wealthy beyond most people's wishes, or quietly respected among their peers, leave a trail of tips from their strategy of accomplishing great feats. These goal qualities separate the goal "DOERS" from the goal "talkers." These are the *Goal DOERS' Winning Qualities* we can learn from by examining the lives of others.

There are five dazzling qualities that *Goal DOERS* possess. They are:

- *Desire*

- *Objective judgment*

- *Elasticity*

- *Resolve, and*

- *Sweat*

DEEP DOWN DEVOTED DESIRE

First, a *deep down devoted desire* is felt by *Goal DOERS*. Why have some notable and ballyhooed national politicians declined running for president although there was a clamor in the media that they would win hands down? New York Governor Mario Cuomo was touted as the best candidate to claim the Democratic nomination for president in 1988. Former basketball star and Senator Bill Bradley was a top pick of the pundits for the Democrats in 1992. Gulf War General Colin Powell was the dream candidate in the Republican race in 1996. What held these terrific goal-achievers from another potential victory? There are many variables that are weighed in such a monumental decision of entering a presidential race. But there was one major component all of these famed "candidates" admitted they lacked at the time. That is *desire*—a "fire in the belly" to seek the nation's highest office. There can be no doubt that each of these famous Americans possessed a great desire to accomplish their individual missions. But at the time these noted leaders names floated on imaginary ballots, they had no deep down devoted desire to be *president.*

Before we venture off on a crusade to conquer our goals, we must first have a burning, passionate craving to accomplish them. Without that commitment and passion, most attempts at leaping toward our goals will likely fall short, and the pursuit will quickly end.

President John F. Kennedy pledged in the early 1960s that before the decade was out, the United States would send a man to the moon and return him safely home again. That profound and ambitious proclamation transformed itself into an intense goal for the country. Many resources, including brains, money, and the lives of dozens of test pilots and three astronauts, were part of the goal's cost. But this bold objective, seemingly a pipe dream from a young, smooth-talking politician, burned in our national belly. And on July 20, 1969, Neil Armstrong set foot on the Sea of Tranquillity declaring, "One small step for man, one giant leap for mankind." Yes, a daring goal can be accomplished, if we have the burning desire to reach it.

Desire to accomplish goals is only the first part of our strategy. As we take action, we must notice our results.

OBJECTIVELY OBSERVING OUR OUTCOMES

Question: What is the definition of insanity?

Answer: Doing the same thing over and over again in exactly the same way but expecting a different result.

Has the following ever happened to us? After sticking the wrong key in a lock and seeing that it is the not the correct one, we try to insert it in the lock again? How many times in our lives do we attempt to, metaphorically speaking, fit a square peg into a round hole? How many times do we face an obstacle placed before us and pretend it does not exist? Perhaps we get negative feedback in a relationship and we ignore it because we do not want to come to terms with the emotional stress?

Even God took time to notice His results. As it says in the Book of Genesis: "On the seventh day God rested, saw what he created, and said that it was good." Many times, even the best intentions of us *Goal DOERS* will lead us to labor and toil pursuing a goal, but never take time to see how far we have come or whether we are heading in the right direction. If it was good enough for God to rest one day of week and observe what He did, then it should be good enough for us.

In Stephen Covey's best-selling book, *The Seven Habits of Highly Effective People,* he tells the story of a man working extremely hard to saw down a tree. The man toils vigorously sawing through the wood, but is making little progress. When advised that he should take a break and sharpen his saw to make the work easier, the man declines, saying he is too busy sawing to sharpen his tool.[52] Are we too busy frantically chasing our dreams to notice if we are making any progress? Are we too concerned with blind activity without "sharpening our saw" by resting, learning, objectively observing, and examining to find whether we are on target?

When we attempt to move forward in our goal plan and take action, we will get some type of result. If the result is not a success, it is also neither a failure nor a defeat. Rather, it is only an outcome. We must recognize that we have not failed. We must accept that it is only an undesired result. Then, we can use the scientific method and use the information to our advantage. We must *objectively observe our outcomes.* Only an objective eye will see where our obstacles lay and our mind will develop paths around the barriers. How do we use negative results to our benefit? Simple. We must try again, but remain adaptable and pliable in the winds of opposition. We must be willing to alter our method by taking the next step.

EMPHASIZE EVER-EVOLVING ELASTICITY

Charles Darwin's Theory of Evolution through natural selection rocked the scientific and the religious world in the second half of the nineteenth century. While avoiding any debate on which method of creation and development should be taught in our schools, there is one finding in Darwin's "survival of the fittest" that can teach us a lesson in successfully reaching our goals. As Darwin theorized, species adapt to their changing environment in order to survive. We must do the same thing if we are to be successful.

How do we do this? By remaining flexible. As mentioned previously, there is no doubt that even if we have a strong desire to accomplish something and work diligently at the task, we will face forces of rejection in our goal-attainment effort. If we take note of our progress, we can make adjustments in direction, tactics, and strategy to stay focused on our purpose.

What is the importance of these mid-course corrections? Would you be surprised to know that a jet plane flying from New York to Los Angeles is off-course most of the time? Or a ship at sea from Boston to London never sails in a completely straight line? Our pursuit of goals is very much like a flying plane or a sailing ship. In a jet plane, the automatic pilot is constantly making adjustments to the plane's direction as wind forces and other atmospheric conditions affect the course. Because the instruments are based on a true compass, the adjustments will keep the aircraft on course. As a sailing ship cuts through the ocean, its pilot makes changes to the craft's rudder and sails to correspond with the forces of wind and water currents. Still, the helmsman keeps a sharp eye on the compass or as in ancient times, the stars, to guide the boat to the intended destination.

Our lives are not much different. As long as we have our own internal "compass," (i.e., our purpose), we will always remain on course if we remain elastic. We need to respond to the forces against us, adjust to the obstacles that lay in our path, and still be willing to take the detours around temporary delays. We will need constant adjustments along the new road of goal-setting. Let's not be afraid to adjust our plans while staying firm in our commitment. We need flexibility when we chase our dreams. A little pliancy will ensure that we will bend, but not break, when faced with the forces of negativism and frustration. We will temporarily bow in the thrust of a hurricane, but we will be still standing when the sun shines again! If we remain stiff and contend that there is only one route to our goal, we are likely to snap in the power of stiff opposition. By remaining flexible, we will ultimately achieve success. We must *emphasize ever-evolving elasticity.*

RIGID RESOLVE REBUFFS REJECTION

While our tactics are flexible, our determination must be rigid. Whether we are competing in an athletic competition or entering a field of battle, it is logical to expect opposition. Very little worthwhile is accomplished without overcoming obstacles. One of the most severe impediments we will face is the mental fear of rejection. A slap of "possible" rejection halts more potential business sales, torpedoes more promising close personal relationships, and stifles more future career developments than any other force or substance known to mankind.

But what is rejection? Is it made of steel? Is it more powerful than a locomotive? Can it leap over and crush all of our dreams in a single bound?

If we are ambitious goal-seekers, we will experience rejection. If we have bold goals, people will criticize us. Those who do not hold our ambition, drive, or mission will turn on us, warning of a million ways how our goals cannot be brought to fruition. Superstars in every profession face rejection at one time or another. Basketball's living legend, Michael Jordan, is unquestionably one of the best that has ever played the game. Yet, he was once cut from his high school basketball team. What would the NBA and the sport of basketball be if Jordan accepted the rejection as a failure and quit the sport? Abraham Lincoln lost numerous election races including the U.S. House of Representatives, Senate, and vice president before he was elected president. What would have happened to the United States during the Civil War without Lincoln's leadership if he decided he was not cut out for politics?

As is the case in many other circumstances, rejection is no more than a detour on our road to determined goals. Rejection is not important. How we react to rejection is critical. We must have *resolve*. We must know how to treat rejection and use the latent benefit that hides inside each temporary setback. Rejection is not defeat. It is only a slight delay. Rejection is not failure. It is only an undesired result. We must know that rigid resolve rebuffs rejection. Rejections are only circumstances. As Adam Smith wrote, "Man is not a creature of circumstances, circumstances are a creature of men."

The ancients said every adversity carries with it a seed of benefit. How many of us as teenagers faced personal rejection when we asked the object of our affection out for a date? Everyone, I would suppose, one time or another. But how many stories are there of those who were persistent in developing a desired relationship and eventually formed a partnership with the person whom initially turned them down? Maybe that happened to you.

How we personally define failure and rejection influences if we will be persistent as *Goal DOERS*. Let's show *rigid resolve* when we encounter the negative forces of rejection and failure. But to reach the finish line, we will not be successful without hard work.

SIZEABLE SOJOURN, SIGNIFICANT SWEAT

A willing to labor long and hard is required for the open job position of *Goal DOERS*. But there is a difference between a trail of drudgery and thankless effort and producing *significant sweat* in the *sizable sojourn* climbing the path to our goal as a labor of love. In a story from the Middle Ages first told by educator Edward Pulling, two workers are asked about their purpose at a building site in France. One worker complained that he was cutting huge boulders with awkward tools—a difficult, backbreaking, and tedious task. Another laborer responded differently when questioned what his work was all about. The second worker said brightly, "I'm building a magnificent cathedral."

We mentioned previously that General Colin Powell had no "burning desire" to be president of the United States. But that does not mean that he did not have a strong desire to accomplish his dreams. And sweat-producing work was an essential component of that. In his autobiography, Powell cites that all work—even his job mopping floors at a bottling plant—is "honorable," no matter what that work is.[53]

There are some excellent resources on the market that can help us discover the job we will love and align both our personality style and desired dreams with an appropriate occupation. But in the short term, if we are in a job that does not correspond directly with our goals and purpose, we can change the *focus* of what we think about. If we cannot love our job, we can love why we are working. If we are employed to save money to provide a certain lifestyle for our family, we can make that the object of our thinking. If we like the purpose of our job and whom it serves, but we do not enjoy the working environment, let's concentrate of who does ultimately benefit from our services. If we are in business, it is the customer. If we are in professional services, it is the client. If we are in medicine, it is the patient. Let's spend more time thinking about how we are serving other people and making a difference for them in our work, and less time with office politics, enduring the boss, or contending with less-than-desirable working conditions.

Becoming an expert in our field involves hard work. We cannot escape it. Olympic Champion Bob Richards said, "You want to be a scholar, you want to be great in the athletic world, you want to be a great statesman, a doctor, a lawyer, anything in life—you want to great in business, in selling—put 10,000 hours of work into it and see what happens in your life!"[54]

In the long term, however, we must come to grips with aligning our service to our designed purpose. If we are not happy in the job that we have, we have the responsibility to change it. However, that does not mean walking into our boss tomorrow and saying, "Take this job and shove it!" When I submitted my first novel to a literary agent, she wisely and warily suggested, "Don't quit your day job." Pragmatism must be exhibited. We can get to where we want to go. We must start deliberately and assuredly, and keep our ultimate job goal in the front of our minds. Before we make the leap to a new job or profession, we should see that there is a safety net below. But, we still will have to take that "leap" if we want to be truly happy with our purpose.

We cannot expect miraculous results overnight. Unlike high school and college finals, we cannot cram the work necessary to achieve lofty goals by making a big pot of coffee and pulling an all-nighter. "As you sow, so shall you reap," the Bible teaches us. We must plant the seeds of our goals in fertile soil. Then we must nourish the ground with proper fertilizer and water our seeds of accomplishment daily. If we care for our crop, we will see a bountiful harvest. True accomplishment results from a well-cared-for field during the entire growing season.

But all this hard work and no play do not have to make us dull boys and girls. Yes, we must pay the price, but we can also enjoy the process as well. This is accomplished by perceiving our work as play.

For many outdoor swinging enthusiasts, the game of golf is the ultimate relaxation. However the great British Prime Minister Winston Churchill once quipped that golf was a game "that involved placing a very small ball into a very small hole with implements ill-designed for the purpose." The difference between work and play is often in the eye of the beholder.

When I was eight years old, every day I went to school I used to pretend that I was actually going to work. For this arduous task, I would pay myself—in play-money of course. It was merely a game of playing "grown-up." Many of our grown-up jobs are very important to society. But they all are part of the game of life. Let's try to make our job a game. When we succeed—sign up a new client, receive a promotion or raise, win employee of the month—let's celebrate! Have a party! When things at work do not go well, let's not despair. Simply, pick up the dice and roll again!

Confucius said, "Choose work you love, and you will never have to work a day in your life." The late author James Michener, who did not begin his prolific writing career until age forty, elaborated: "The master in the art of living makes little distinction between his work and his play, his labor and his leisure his mind and his body, his information and his recreation, his love and his religion. He hardly knows which is which. He simply pursues his vision of excellence at whatever he does, leaving others to decide whether he is working or playing. To him he's always doing both."

Goal DOERS do not work 9 to 5. *Goal DOERS* work evenings, weekends, and burn the midnight oil. This does not mean we knock our lives out of balance and ignore other important roles and relationships we have. But it does mean that our identified goal takes a high priority, and we concentrate on it. A 1998 survey of Americans found that 83 percent felt that hard work was very important to the American character. Only 31 percent felt money was.[55] Do not quit the pursuit. It is only a game, and our purpose should be to play it well. We might not always win, but it is lots of fun when we do. And we cannot win if we do not play.

Winning *Goal DOERS* like us hold a *deep down devoted desire* to achieve our goals, *objectively observe our outcomes, emphasize ever-evolving elasticity* in our options for achievement, *rebuff rejection* through *rigid resolve* when faced with disappointment, and generate *significant sweat* in our *sizeable sojourn* as we work hard toward our goals. These characteristics make all of us smarter, stronger, and successful *Goal DOERS*. But as we go further in our quest for a sturdy house of goals, we must constantly practice the *ABC Strategies of Success.*

12

The ABC Strategies of Success

Abcdefghijklmnopqrstuvwxyz is the funniest-looking word I've ever seen.
—Big Bird

So far, we have selected a firm foundation for our house of goals by carving out our personal purpose. We have selected the materials to build our own home of goals by aligning our value structure and our supportive positive belief systems. Then, we drew a blueprint of what goals we want to achieve. Now we have a location, materials, and a plan. It looks like we are ready to start building our dreams. But before we hammer the first nail or place the first board on our foundation, we must make sure our carpenters, contractors, and architects are all qualified and in agreement with our wishes. We want to insure that these professionals are among the best available. Who are these individuals? *They* are us.

This chapter is a list of principles, qualities, values, and practices that will be helpful to complete this construction project smoothly and without major conflicts. These twenty-six qualities, listed in no particular order other than they follow the alphabet to help us remember them, are all-important. They are essential to make sure our house is constructed in good order. What would happen if we built our house and the contractor did not talk to the architect who designed it? What would happen if we used expensive materials but selected a shoddy carpenter with poor craftsmanship? What if we built our house beautifully but discovered when we were finished that we forgot to install the plumbing? I guess we then build an outhouse! On a cold winter morning, we would regret not taking a closer look at our plans before construction.

Finely built homes work as a system. The landscaping complements the home's design. The windows are intended to absorb the sun's energy in winter, but shades repel the blistering heat of summer. A properly designed heating and cooling system will keep us comfortable all year round. For homeostasis, or balance, a home's atmosphere must be treated as a system. Each room blends into another, a perfect place for living, relaxing, dining, sleeping, and playing. The ancient Chinese art of Feng Shui—a system of environmental placement—is gaining popularity for this very reason.

Our daily living also works best when it is part of a carefully selected and meticulously practiced system. There are a number of analogies that can compare how all our experiences and daily habits work best when they are coordinated with upright, effective principles. We can compare ourselves to a complicated machine that produces intricate work, in which even the smallest part out of alignment can throw the whole massive process off kilter. Our performance can be affected by the "butterfly effect." Author James Gleick refers to the concept that theorizes that the flapping of a butterfly's wings in one part of the world can affect major weather patterns in another part of the world.[56] Similarly, if we are incongruent with our purpose in one role in our life, it can affect all of our roles. We can equate our lives with the performance of a sports team, which requires the firm balance of numerous positions and skills working efficiently before a winning game plan can be executed. Can we imagine a successful football team with a terrific defense, but a weak quarterback and offense that does not score any points? Can we picture a home-run happy baseball team without any pitching or field defense to protect its lead? Without the balance of skills, the team is sure to be a loser. We can liken ourselves to a farmer, or gardener, who must regularly nourish and water the planted seeds in fertile soil to wield a healthy crop after a long growing season. The slightest neglect in the process could result in a ruined harvest and a lot of wasted effort.

For those of us in business, we can relate our goal-setting process to a corporation. We are the corporation of living that includes the chief executive officer (CEO), the stockholders, the customers, the employees, and the managers. We are all "self-employed" in our life, trying to produce a quality product (our accomplishments) and provide a service (our lives) that benefit others, and turn a profit (a life worth living).

The *CEO* of our life outlines the purpose of our organization and sets corresponding goals. The *manager* organizes our actions to achieve clear objectives and measures our progress. The *employees* work hard to produce the product or provide the service. The *customer* sees the fruits of our labor by enjoying what we contribute in life. And finally, the *stockholder*—that's us too, folks—is richer for the effort.

It is often said that if government were run like a business, it would operate more efficiently and effectively. The same can be true for our lives. If we run our own lives as efficiently and effectively as we do our businesses, we would probably be happier people who accomplish great feats. Our lives are no ordinary profit-minded corporation, however. We are a corporation with a worthy purpose that provides useful products and services to benefit others. This, in turn, enriches our own lives. The following principles can ensure that our building corporation constructs not only a sturdy house of goals, but also a loving home welcome to everyone that visits.

A) *Attitude*

The greatest discovery of my generation is that a human being can alter his life by altering his attitudes of mind.—William James

There is no coincidence that the most vital attribute to successful goal-achievers begins with the letter A for *Attitude*. Without a confident, hopeful, and highly expectant attitude, there can be no affirmative belief. Without affirmative belief, there is no positive vision. Without a positive vision, there is no *long-term* effective action. Without effective action there are no favorable results. Therefore, a positive, but constructive attitude is necessary to grease the axle of action, or the *Goal Motivation Wheel* cannot spin freely. Psychologist and best-selling author Dr. Wayne Dyer says, "There is no way to happiness. Happiness *is* the way."[57] In other words, we cannot wait or search for the elusive experience of contentment before we take positive action in our lives. We must adopt and express an attitude of joy and hopeful expectancy first. Then we are on the right road to a worthy destination.

Have you ever been on an elevator and asked a coworker or friend, "How are you?" The response we get is, "Okay...for a Monday!" or "Since it's payday, I'm doing all right." Do we, living in the freest nation on the earth and capable of doing practically anything we want, live a life of such total drudgery that we have to depend on Friday afternoon at five o'clock or a paycheck slipped into our hands to experience joy?

Try this. The next time someone asks us, "How's it going?" when they see us in the morning, proclaim, "Fantastic!" or "Tremendous!" or "This is the greatest day of my life!" While our friends will look at us a little peculiar and wonder if we stopped by the neighborhood pub on the way to work, we will experience a curious emotion. We will feel a bit more optimistic. Even if we had a flat tire on the way to work, our dog just died, and our head is swimming from the flu, the seemingly phony exclamation that we are doing just "great" triggers our mind to create positive emotions to justify our statement. This may not be possible if we are experiencing genuine tragedy in our lives. But most of the time, things are flowing along smoothly and while we apathetically say our life is "fair," our minds then accept it as a boring rut. We can "fool" our mind into thinking we are feeling better than we may think. Before long, if we continue to claim that we are doing great, or at least, better than average, we may actually start believing it. Let's not trudge through life feeling "okay;" let's be "SanFrantastic!"

Here is another tip to improve our attitude. Do we watch the local and national television news every evening? Don't. That is heresy coming from a former broadcast journalist like myself. Today's broadcast news is polluted with nothing but the latest tragedy, warnings, and stories laden with more moral depravation than ever before. According to psychology expert Dr. Daniel Goleman, studies of heavy television watchers have discovered that these individuals are generally more depressed after watching the tube than before they started watching.[58] And to top it all off, most of the tales of woe have absolutely no impact on our own daily lives. Television broadcasters tell us that they are giving the public what they want to see. But when I go to a restaurant, I do not ask for the spoiled food they are throwing in the dumpster behind the building be put on my plate. And that is exactly what the majority of "interesting" news is being served to us every evening for dinner.

During my stint as a journalist I was a news junkie. I listened to radio news constantly and read a dozen newspapers daily. I watched the local television news broadcasts and then followed it up with Dan, Tom, and Peter on the national scene. When that was over, I tuned in CNN, just in case I missed something. Although I would absorb a trickle of useful knowledge in the avalanche of information, the bulk of the empty calorie news diet just gave me a bad attitude of indigestion. Child abuse, the shaky economy, wars in Asia, the Middle East, and Africa, a polluted environment, rip-off businesses, wife-killers, movie-star divorces—who needs it? Who could be happy and positive while so much misfortune and tragedy exist in the world? One day, I turned it off, and an amazing thing happened. I felt happier. Instead of seeing the problems of the day, I began doing something about them by volunteering in the community in my own small way. Instead of ruminating over the problems, I became a small part of the solution.

If we think we are missing out on the critical information we need to know, think again. Most of the things we hear about on the news are items of which we will discover that we have absolutely no control. Let's spend our time becoming involved in things in which we do have control. Go on news diet. Read one or two good newspapers daily, catch a radio broadcast or tune into a significant interview of interest on TV. Do not overdose. Also, examine each source with a critical eye and ear. Remember that a glutton's portion of ratings-oriented news broadcasts will give us nothing but an information ache and clogged positive arteries. Take it from someone who used to serve and consume that slop! Too much is not good for us.

OPPORTUNITY:

Name one debilitating attitude and what new energizing attitude you will adopt.

B) *Belief*

The mind can hold only one idea at a time.—Mark Twain

If Samuel Longhorn Clemens (a.k.a. Mark Twain) was right, why do we often choose to fill our mind with a negative thought? While we dwell on the less-than-desired forecasts and nightmare scenarios that are only imagined possibilities, the positive beliefs and dreams have no room in God's greatest invention—our brain. Let's insert a positive *belief* in that single thinking slot instead of a negative one. Negative thoughts can only be a prescription for unsatisfactory results. Dr. Norman Vincent Peale gave us *The Power of Positive Thinking* years ago. Isn't it time we adopted it?

Although naysayers dispute the claim that positive thinking will yield success, it most assuredly will provide better results than negative thinking. A 2002 study in Europe revealed that positive thinking did not help cancer patients live longer. But the researchers admit that psychological approaches did help patients *cope* with their disease.[59] That is all we can ask. Other research finds different results. In addition to forwarding our goals, positive thinking is linked to health benefits as well by enabling people to meet stressful events in their life with better resources. According to recent research, optimistic people appear to have less heart disease, mental health problems, and recover faster from surgery.[60]

The best way to empirically test the impact of positive thinking is to try it. But remember positive thinking will not change the forces of nature, or the actions of other people. What it will do is dictate the "reaction" we have to the events that occur around us. If we view a devastating event as only an occurrence, it will not change the outcome of the calamity, nor will it necessarily remove the emotional suffering we experience as a result of it. However, it will open our minds up to the possibility of options to recover from practically any disaster that happens to us. We have heard the expressions "If it ain't fatal, then don't worry about it," and "Don't sweat the small stuff, and it's all small stuff."

Let's not dwell on what happened or what *may* happen. Let's concentrate on what we *can* make happen. And it begins with a positive *belief* system.

OPPORTUNITY:

Name one negative belief you will cast out and one positive belief you will substitute in its place.

C) *Consistency*

Practice yourself what you preach.—Titus Maccius Plautus

Why do we brush our teeth? Well, of course, it prevents cavities, keeps our mouth clean and free of disease, and helps us avoid halitosis. But does brushing our teeth once in a while accomplish the same goal?

Certainly not, any oral hygienist will tell us. We must brush our teeth everyday, at least twice a day, or perhaps after every meal if we can. So, only the consistent and regular brushing of teeth will yield the results we want. And don't forget to floss!

Consistency—practicing the fundamentals as often as possible—will yield excellent results. National Basketball Association Hall of Fame star Larry Bird of the Boston Celtics once filmed a soft-drink television commercial. In the short advertisement, Bird, an exceptional outside shooter, was to intentionally *miss* a shot. It took the basketball star numerous takes before he successfully missed a shot on purpose! Bird was such a consistent accurate shooter, he had to concentrate very hard just to miss!

Another famous sports star displays this consistent effort. Tony Gywnn of the San Diego Padres won more major league batting titles in modern baseball history than any other player did. He consistently batted over a .300 average, the threshold identified as the level for an excellent hitter. How did Gwynn reach this elevated level? Just innate talent? Much more than that. He never stopped hitting. While the baseball season lasts from April to September, Gwynn practiced hitting every single day of the year, except for a two-week vacation with his family. If he could not make it to the ballpark batting cage, he practiced hitting balls against a rug hanging in his garage. No wonder when the game was on the line, the most dangerous hitter a pitcher could face was Tony Gwynn.

As we travel through life, we often notice that those people who enjoy a notable reputation are those who consistently treat others well. Those who have the opposite notoriety are known for "biting your head off" when things are not going well for them, or just plain "moody." "Don't get the in boss's way today," the secretary exclaims, "he's in one of *those* moods." Is it any wonder that *those* people do not enjoy a pleasant reputation even though they might treat others fairly a portion of the time? We are not necessarily judged by how we act when things are going well, but rather, how we act when things are going poorly. How we consistently respond to others matters more than the few times we may be exceptionally pleasant. If we show true interest and kindness to other people on a consistent basis, we will have the type of reputation we desire.

It is possible to change how others perceive us and how we appreciate ourselves. But it takes consistency of action to build up our personal integrity. If we desire to be winning goal achievers as well, we must act consistently.

OPPORTUNITY:

Name one consistent behavior of goal-achievers that you will exhibit in the future.

D) *Discipline*

Discipline is the soul of an army. It makes small numbers formidable; procures success to the weak, and esteem to all.—George Washington

In order to exhibit the type of consistency described above and routinely produce reliable results, we also need the *discipline* of Larry Bird or Tony Gywnn. Self-sacrifice and self-denial are part of discipline conditioning required to create the dependable results of our goal-striving efforts. The famous pianist Arthur Rubinstein once commented on why he had to practice his musical skills on a daily basis. "If I miss one day," Rubinstein reportedly said, "I notice. If I miss two days, the conductor notices. If I miss three days, the audience notices."

How disciplined are we as we practice, rehearse, and steadily climb up the goal ladder? Any major professional sports coach will tell us that the practicing of the fundamentals is necessary if we are to be competitive. Repetition *is* the mother of skill. Famed professional football coach Don Shula says, "over preparing" was necessary for his players to have the winning edge.[61] Competitors must know their plays backwards and forwards before walking on the field on game day, says Shula, who, by the way, has more wins than any other professional football coach in history, including an unduplicated National Football League perfect winning season.

A critical component of practice and discipline is the steady advancement of our skills. The Japanese, who copied and perfected the making of steel, automobiles, and electronics, wrestled these major industries from United States' dominance. They have a term for this discipline. It is called "Kaisen." Translated, it means "constant and never-ending improvement." By taking constant action towards our goal, and making definite steps—not necessarily leaps—in improvement each day, we will soon find ourselves on top of the heap. But even once reaching that level, we cannot stop there. We can never stand still in life. We are either going forward in our progression toward our goals and purpose or we are going backward. If we tread water, we will be passed backwards down the stream by a steady current. To continually move ahead, we must constantly keep swimming (i.e., improve our beliefs, efforts, actions, and results).

OPPORTUNITY:

Write down several things you need to be more disciplined about and ways you can increase your commitment to improve your skills.

E) *Energy*

Beware of rashness, but with energy and sleepless vigilance go forward and give us victories.—Abraham Lincoln

If we have set ambitious goals for ourselves, we will obviously need the mental drive as well as physical force to motor us forward. Without an abundant source of energy, our starry ideas to boldly go where we have never gone before will never get off the ground.

A recent report on obesity in the United States determined that a lack of exercise was a major cause of America's overweight problem. As my teenage kids would say, "No, duuuuuhhhh!" Is it any surprise that we are one of the most obese societies on earth when our national pastime is eating in front of the television night and day? Today's new opium-like addictions of surfing the Internet without a concrete goal, playing endless video games, and viewing a bottomless pit of videotapes, DVDs, satellite channels, and reality TV are not only the obsession of our youth. Many adults stay glued to the boob tube or the video screen until their eyes bug out and their bodies collapse from inactivity. How can we expect to be *Super Goal-Achievers*, avoid speeding bullets of negativity, have more personal power than a locomotive, and leap over tall objectives with a single bound with an empty fuel tank? Television and overdosing on the Internet is today's *Kryptonite* for us Clark Kents. A little may not hurt, but too much of a dose is terminal, no pun intended. Avoid it, goal-makers of steel. Use these powerful communication tools wisely. Watch intelligent television (you will have to search hard) and have a defined goal in seeking information on the Web.

We not only must have a proper diet to create our own energy, but we also need a regular mental *and* physical exercise program. With our senses dulled with soap operas, droll and perverse television talk shows, and hours of annoying commercials, it is no wonder many of us cannot sharpen our thinking and contemplate exciting goals. With poor diets, no regular exercise habits, and a lack of sleep exacerbated by watching late-night television, are we astonished that attempts to work the extra hours to realize our dreams are so difficult without the needed amount of energy?

Another Ben Franklin maxim is: "Early to bed, early to rise, makes one healthy, wealthy, and wise." That old saw has stuck for more than 200 years because it is true. *First*, we need the proper rest and sleep to be a lean, mean, goal-setting machine. That means a few hours less in the taverns of the town and missing a few one-liners from Jay and David, but at least we will be rested enough to begin our daily hunt of fulfilling objectives.

Second, we must keep our minds as active as possible. We need to spend less time listening to the endless dribble of the top-forty radio stations and insulting disc jockeys and more time honing our thinking skills by researching our areas of interest. This can include browsing our local library, controlled use of the World Wide Web, and listening to educational audiotapes/CDs.

Third, a regular physical fitness program will not only shed those ugly pounds we continually complain about, but it will also increase the value of our rest, stimulate our thinking capacity, and create more energy than we have ever experienced before. It has been demonstrated that physical activity stimulates endorphins (our body's natural and soothing opiate) in the brain. This can lead to increased and clearer thinking. That is why many intellectuals enjoy a good walk during periods of study. It helps contribute to better comprehension.

It is important for us to find an activity that we enjoy, or any exercise program we invest in may be money and effort down the drain. Although most physical fitness experts will tell us that there are endless physical, mental, spiritual, and social benefits from aerobic and strength training, some studies suggest that exercise can actually have negative effects if the person does not enjoy it. What do you enjoy? Walking? Running? Swimming? Biking? Volleyball? Yoga? It matters more that we like what we are doing, than what activity we do. Because if we do not find pleasure in the activity, chances are we will quit.

The self-help movement of getting into shape is a multi-billion dollar business in the United States. However, many of us spend more time thinking about our physical exercise than actually doing it! The proof? Most exercise equipment is advertised on TV! Why don't more people exercise? Of course we know! It's painful! Our minds will devise any plan or excuse to run away from pain, remember? We are not that dumb! However, we must recall the *Goal Motivation Wheel*. If we wait for the uphill motivation, the wheel will probably never turn because the laws of physics (and pain!) are against us. Motivation is analogous to Kevin Costner's character in the movie *Field of Dreams*. Wondering why anyone would come to a baseball field in the middle of an Iowa cornfield, Costner's character received a spiritual message. "If you build it, they will come," was the directive he heard in his head. In the case of motivation, "If we act, the motivation will come." We have to take action first, achieve a result, and then the motivation will follow.

Do not wait to "get motivated." Get moving instead and the motivation will arrive on schedule. And if we say, "Well, my schedule doesn't permit me to get away during the day to work out and I'm too busy at home, and, and, and…" Beware, that is only an EXCUSE. I have exercised at ten o'clock at night after putting my children to bed, or at seven o'clock in the morning because that was my only free time available. We will never *find* the time. But we can *make* the time; it does not matter when we do it. Let's do it to fit our own schedule. And we do not have to compete in triathlons to build an exercise regimen. Many new studies show that moderate exercise—walking briskly for thirty minutes five times a week—has significant health benefits. If we can walk instead of driving somewhere, make that our exercise time. If we can walk the stairs instead of staring at the wall and not talking to anyone in an elevator, let's do it. We need to walk, run, or play, whenever we can fit it in. The energy that it creates will fill our power tank to fuel our goal journey every single day.

OPPORTUNITY:

List several physical activities that you enjoy that can bring better health and energy.

Map out a plan of regular exercise in your ordinary day. Many physicians recommend thirty minutes of aerobic activity at least five times a week. As always, check with your doctor before you begin an exercise program.

List several healthy foods you can integrate into your diet.

F) *Focus*

If one advances confidently in the direction of his dreams, and endeavors to live the life which he has imagined, he will meet with a success unexpected in common hours.—Henry David Thoreau

When I was a young boy, lazy, hazy summer afternoons would often get boring. So, as young children do from time to time, I would tend to engage in a little mischief. My friends and I would take a magnifying glass from my brother's biology kit and enter the back-alley laboratory for a little fun. On a bright sunny day, we would use the magnifying power of the glass to converge the sun's rays to burn a hole through paper, dry leaves, and even toast ants crawling across the pavement (yuck, that's sick!). Though one may wonder about my compassion for insects, I did learn a bit about focus.

Sunlight, as I already knew, could be comfortably warm. *Focused* sunlight, on the other hand, could be downright deadly. At least, if you are an ant. Can we use our minds to focus our laser beam concentration toward our goals? Of course we can! When we have selected our most important goals, we cannot let them out of our minds for one day. That is the purpose of writing and reviewing our goals on a daily basis. Motivational author Rich Fettke in his book *Extreme Success* says focus creates powerful momentum that moves us forward. Constant attention and thought focused on our objectives will result in true progress toward them.[62]

Watch out, however, because negative focus can be equally powerful as positive focus. The sun's amplified heat can cause destruction by setting fire to combustible objects. Pessimistic focus can drill a hole through our plans and sink our goals. Optimistic focus, on the other hand, holds the strength to freeze the fires of gloom and melt the ice of the impossible. Let's focus strongly on our goals with pragmatic optimism and watch the fire!

OPPORTUNITY:

Describe how you will increase the focus of at least one of your goals:

G) *Goals*

Dream lofty dreams, and as you dream, so shall you become.—James Allen

It seems redundant to stress the importance of goals at this point in a book dedicated to accomplishing them. But here are few other things to keep in mind:

First, *goals equal control*. What we are really after in life is not necessarily the accomplishment of fantastic goals, but to achieve a satisfying level of happiness, contentment, and peace with ourselves. According to some studies, many of those surveyed equated their happiness with the amount of control they felt they had in their lives. The more control over their own life, the more contented they were. Are we pursuing our own goals? Chances are, if we are not working for our own goals, we are working for someone else's. Let's take responsibility of our goals and therefore gain control over our life. That way, happiness will be our own.

Second, goal-setting is *fun*. This process is not realized by thinking weak wishes and throwing a penny in the well. Goal construction is watching previews of coming attractions in the theater of our mind's eye. The more exciting we make the previews of upcoming events, the more intense we will make those dreams come true in our own personal life movie. And we are the screenwriter, the producer, the director, and the star.

H) *Habit*

Habits are like a cable. We weave a strand of it everyday and soon it cannot be broken.—Horace Mann

The late Earl Nightingale once said that if we want to find out where a person will be five or ten years from now, take a look at how that person is spending his or her time today. The habits we create and maintain this day will determine what type of person we will be far in the future. Let's take a look at our daily habits. What are we spending our time doing? What do we do consistently? It is no secret that the habits that we developed five or more years ago determine how we currently think, act, and feel now. If we began an exercise program several years ago that we adhered to, we are probably in reasonably good physical condition. If we have regularly studied and kept abreast of the new developments within our chosen career field, we are prepared for the changes that lie ahead.

Let's take a look at our daily routine and commit to create changes in our regular habits to benefit us far in the future. We will get some immediate results and that's good, but satisfying payoffs will have to wait. But if we are disciplined, the fruit of our labors will be sweet.

OPPORTUNITY:

List three habits that will positively move you toward your goals:

1.

2.

3.

I) *Imaging positively*

Let there be light.—God

In the beginning, there was the Word. Did you ever notice that in the Book of Genesis, God *spoke* the world into existence? If we believe that a higher power created our world, is it possible that God imagined the earth before its formation? This shines a little light on the power of *imaging positively*.

Recall the story of the frustrated golfer who hits a bad shot and says, "I knew I was going to do that!" Often, we mentally rehearse a negative outcome to our actions. As Napoleon Hill's research on successful people revealed, "The mind attracts what it concentrates on." Therefore, if we think only negative outcomes to our actions, our impartial subconscious will try to reach that end. Conversely, the opposite can be true. A 1999 study cited in the *Personality and Social Psychology Bulletin* found that students who mentally simulated the process of doing well on a test actually did perform better.[63]

To help us reach our goals, the use of positive imaging can achieve desired results. The story of Michelangelo's statue of David is a good example of imaging. Using a slab of stone that was rejected by other stonecutters, Michelangelo chipped away at the block until he created his famous masterpiece. The artist claimed that the statue was already in the stone. He only chipped away everything that did not look like it. He imagined the beautiful work of art before he picked up his hammer and chisel. Walt Disney's brother Roy explained that although his famous brother died before the opening of Epcot Center in Disney World, he did get a chance to see it. "Walt saw it and that's why you are seeing it," Roy Disney claimed. "He was a visionary." Walt even imagined what others said could not be done. "It's kind of fun to do the impossible," Walt once said.

When we use positive imaging, we must play an active role. I have used it in my own life, and have been astounded how a vivid image in my mind would be remarkably similar to the actual achievement of a goal I set months, sometimes years earlier. If we are imagining that we are accomplishing the great task we have always dreamed about, should we view it from a third person point-of-view, watching someone exactly like us walking up to the podium, being honored for our great achievement? Or, should we see it out of our own mind's eye, conceiving every moment as we would actually feel it? I submit that it would be much more effective if we rehearse the image as we would experience it rather than observe it as a fly on the wall. And some researchers agree. Writing in the *Journal of Personality,* German researchers Oliver C. Schultheiss and Joachim C. Brunstein stated that, "engaging in goal imagery helps a person realize what it would mean to strive for a specific goal by experiencing how emotionally satisfying its pursuit and attainment would be for him or her."[64] That way, we can experience our vision first hand and feel the thrilling emotion of accomplishing our goal even before we start our journey. That personal vision will make our goal believable and will be a tonic of motivation that will fire us up and shoot us toward the stars.

OPPORTUNITY:

Describe in vivid detail what it would feel like to reach your goal. What would you see? What would you hear? Who would be there with you?

J) *Journey*

The soul of a journey is liberty, perfect liberty, to think, feel, do, just as one pleases.—William Hazlitt

Despite all the information about the importance of goals in our lives, what does it all mean anyway? Whatever we accomplish in our lives, we are on a train that has the same destination: death! Does it really matter how many mountains we climb, how many sales we achieve, or how much money we make? I love the bumper sticker that says, "Whoever dies with the most toys, wins!" Since we are on the same train that begins with birth, navigates a complete circle and ends where we started (that is, non-human existence), we may conclude that it is not the destination, but rather, the *journey* is the real meaning of life.

Some research claims that men are more goal-oriented, while women are more concerned with the quality of the relationships they form in life. We could probably come up with couples that fit the opposite description. But just as it takes both men and women to make life thrive and perpetuate, it takes goals *and* relationships to make the world go round.

Imagine this married couple: the "goal-oriented" woman and the relationship-oriented man who go on an ocean cruise. Can the goal-oriented wife see the logic of taking an ocean cruise that goes around in a circle and comes back to the starting point? "What have we accomplished?" she would boast. "We went around in a circle, but we didn't get anywhere!"

However, the "relationship-oriented" husband gets back from the trip and says, "What a great trip we had!" Perhaps our life can be compared to a cruise. But when we are on it, let's not concern ourselves with the destination, let's just enjoy the trip.

J can also represent the word *Journal* as well as *Journey*. The most exciting autobiography we will ever read is our own. Today, let's begin a journal to track our progress. Keep a journal to log goals and deadlines, reasons for going after our dreams, and comments and thoughts as we pursue and accomplish our objectives. A journal is not a diary. A journal is a living document that assists us in the goal-setting and goal-accomplishing process. Any life worth living is worth recording.

OPPORTUNITY:

Write the first entry of your journal here and later transfer it to a separate volume.

K) *Knowledge*

An investment in knowledge pays the best interest.—Benjamin Franklin

He should know. Franklin created the first post office, the first library, an Ivy League University, an experiment harnessing electricity, etc. He conceived of paratroopers, invented bifocals, and spent his life in vocations as a printer, diplomat, statesman, writer, philosopher, economist, and a linguist who understood five languages. Yeah, I know, he couldn't hold a job.

Like Franklin, who read and studied his entire life, we must fill our heads with healthy positive ideas and worthy knowledge. We will not reach our target by positive thinking alone.

One way to increase the amount of knowledge we absorb is to increase our reading speed. Shockingly, recent surveys show that the amount of reading Americans do—pathetically little—is declining even further! Many times, we do not bother to start a book, let alone finish it, because it just takes too long to read. Also available at the library is any one of numerous speed-reading courses that can both increase the rate of our reading and can actually improve our comprehension. Speed-reading is easier than we may imagine—all it takes is concentration and practice. Speed-reading will reincarnate our desire to read and seek out new information that we have ignored in the past.

Anything we have ever wanted to know is available at our local library, thanks to the institution Franklin started. And it is all available to us at little or no cost. Not enough time to read? As I mentioned earlier in this book, the audiotape/CD will make our home chores and commuting time turn into our personal institute of higher learning. Enroll today for free and take advantage of it!

OPPORTUNITY:

List three books you have intended to read to help you toward your goals and read them!

1.

2.

3.

L) *Love*

Whatever the question, love is the answer.—Wayne Dyer

I mentioned earlier that one reason many people do not pursue their goals is because of fear. Coincidentally, fear happens to be the direct opposite of love. Nothing works for the better without love. The world-famous friend of the hungry and poor and soon to be saint, the late Mother Teresa of Calcutta, said, "There is more hunger for love and appreciation in this world than for bread." When there is complete love in our life, there is no room for fear. When there is total caring in our world there is no need for resentment towards others. When there is undiminished forgiveness in our life, there is no need for blame. As the famous "love doctor" Leo Buscaglia, claimed, the lack of trust and forgiveness are key impediments of a loving relationship.[65]

Often, the lack of forgiveness we have for others acts as a roadblock to our goals. Brian Tracy, in his book *Maximum Achievement*, gives a simple three-step power forgiveness formula for blasting this roadblock out of our way:[66]

- *Step 1: Forgive your Parents.* How many of us spend precious hours, days, weeks, or years blaming our mothers and fathers for all of our current troubles? Our parents did the best they could with the knowledge and resources they had to raise us properly. They were not perfect; nor are we. By forgiving our parents, we accept the responsibility for our own goals and our lives.

- *Step 2: Forgive Yourself.* Speaking of wasted time. When we make mistakes and things do not turn out as planned, many of us blame ourselves. Worse than that, we have trouble forgiving ourselves for being human. Fine, but didn't I just state that we should not blame our parents' upbringing for our current situation, and accept our own accountability for the direction of our lives? Yes, but *responsibility is not blame*. Blame is a tactic to avoid responsibility. Or, when we accept it and do not absolve ourselves, our motivation to go forward is stuck in a mire of self-criticism. We can accept responsibility for undesired results as we move ahead toward our goals. We possess the spiritual power to pardon ourselves for not being perfect and move on. It is by granting this freedom can we truly be unencumbered from the cursing shackles of blame and self-censure.

- *Step 3: Forgive Everyone Else.* Since we are getting pretty good at the forgiveness thing, we might as well go all the way. Have we ever committed any of these blame acts: Denouncing the boss for our dead-end job; blaming the checkout clerk at the grocery store for a slow-moving line; cursing another driver for cutting us off in traffic; reproaching our children for being an ungrateful burden; etc? Has blaming anyone else for our misfortune ever added a day to our lives? Has bearing a grudge against a person improved the quality of our life in the long run? Has withholding forgiveness from a person seeking it made us sleep better? Forgiveness is the basis of the love God has for us. Forgiveness not only creates love in our lives, but it also frees us from the burden of resentment that impedes our growth. Sometimes forgiveness is a difficult task if we have faced an unjust wrong. But most wonderful things in life can only be achieved with a little struggle.

Forgiveness, however, is easier than we think. All it takes is an open mind and an open heart.

OPPORTUNITY:

List three people you need to forgive to remove these awkward burdens from your shoulders.

1.

2.

3.

M) *Modeling*

Imitation is the sincerest of flattery.—Charles Caleb Colton

When I was a young boy, I could mimic every batting stance of the starting line-up of the 1971 World Champion baseball team, the Pittsburgh Pirates. Playing whiffle ball in my backyard in inner-city Pittsburgh, I would strike the professional pose of the late Hall-of-Famer Roberto Clemente or the home-run slugger Willie Stargell. Did copying the batting stance make me a better hitter? No, not exactly. But it gave a shot to my enthusiasm for the game by modeling my sports heroes.

When we want to climb toward significant goals in our life, most likely, we are not the first person to pursue that summit. There are only a few people like Jonas Salk, Martin Luther King Jr., or Amelia Earhart. If we are chasing after a dream that has been accomplished before, why start from scratch to discover a successful strategy? Let's look to those who have achieved our definition of success and model ourselves after them. This is not copying or plagiarizing. We are simply using an effective tactic to reach a successful result. By using winning examples as our models, we can make the road to fruition a little smoother and avoid the potholes others may have struck. Sooner or later, we will edge our own groove and others will use us as the model to pattern themselves after.

A perfect example of "mass modeling" is the recovery of post-war Japan. After near total destruction of industrial capacity by American bombing during World War II, the Japanese economy rose out of the ashes and within four decades dominated major industries once commanded by American business. How did they do this? By applying Shintoism to industrialization? No, they copied the United States economic system. With the help of American business minds, they changed the perception of "Made in Japan" as an American slur for "cheap and unreliable" to the world's model of quality. A primary American mentor for the Japanese, the late Dr. Edward Deming, achieved the most notoriety as a model. After the war, Deming, a statistician, taught Japanese businessmen his fourteen quality points including the issues of purpose, perseverance, on-the-job training, self-improvement, breaking barriers, driving out fear, creating trust in the business environment, and, of course, constant and never-ending improvement.[67] Sounds a lot like the Japanese term "Kaisen" discussed earlier, doesn't it? By using these methods to improve production policy, and by setting clear, achievable goals to produce the finest quality products, the Japanese first targeted the American steel industry. This was followed by systematic moves into the automobile industry, and finally, electronic equipment. Ironically, in the 1980s, Japanese methods—formed by Dr. Deming's teachings—became the model for the resurgence of the American product quality movement. The models were modeling the modelers!

All of these accomplishments were based on modeling. Americans have more modern inventions to their credit in many highly technological businesses than any other country. But the Japanese proved they are the best modelers on the planet. Modeling is a powerful goal-achievement device that we can pull out of our toolbox at any time.

OPPORTUNITY:

Name three models you can use for inspiration, knowledge, and guidance toward your goals.

1.

2.

3.

N) *No Excuses*

The greater the obstacle, the more glory in overcoming it.—Moliere

No Excuses is another term for accepting responsibility. We must accept responsibility for our own goals and our own lives. And as we meet obstacles along the way, we cannot levy blame or avoid accountability. There may be legitimate and unavoidable reasons for unsuccessful attempts as we move ahead toward our goals, but if we want to achieve success, we cannot offer rationalizations. We simply need to change our tactics and try again.

President Harry S. Truman may have faced more critical decisions during his presidency than any other modern president. The monumental global issues included: dropping the atomic bomb on Japan to end World War II; the reconstruction of war-torn Europe; rebuilding of the peacetime American economy; mounting a near impossible re-election bid; and managing the stalemate war in Korea that potentially could have developed into World War III. But it is not always the results of his presidential decisions that are remembered by students of history today. What is often remembered from "Give 'em Hell, Harry," is the plaque on his desk that read, "The Buck Stops Here." All bucking of responsibility ended with him. Though Truman's popularity numbers while in office were much lower than many modern presidents, he is now fondly respected and remembered for accepting the responsibility of the burdens of his high position and carrying out his duties honorably and honestly. That is what makes goal-achievers powerful. Accept no excuses. Impose no blame. Embrace responsibility and do not surrender to obstacles in our path.

OPPORTUNITY:

What excuses have you been using to keep yourself from pursuing your goals?

O) *Organization*

We can…lay plans as if we were to be immortal; and we find then that these words do make a genuine difference in our moral life.—William James

"By failing to plan, you are planning to fail." That oft-turned phrase is common in business today, and in effective goal-setting, it applies just as much. The major reason we do fail to plan is because it takes time—time we think we do not have in our always-busy schedules. Planning is often looked at as non-productive because we are not generating anything tangible from the time spent plotting strategy. But this is a shortsighted view. Without proper organization and planning, we will be soon off-course and aimless and then we must spend a gargantuan amount of time trying to find our path again.

Managing time is a top business priority and the subject of dozens of books, seminars, and training classes. Before we look at managing our time, we have to take a look at what time is in the first place. Time, it has been said in jest, is God's way of preventing everything from happening at once. Humor aside, that statement is quite logical. Have we ever had a day that we had so many things to accomplish we became overwhelmed, and as a result, accomplished very little? That is usually the result of a failure to plan our time appropriately. But what about the unexpected "fires" that arise in our lives every day that must be put out? Who can account for that? And what about the laundry list of things that must be done on a daily basis? If we consume all of our available time accomplishing tasks, when do we have time to relax? When can we recharge our batteries to face the next day of endless tasks before us? The job! The kids! The laundry!

Don't we have enough time? Well, we must come to the realization that we have all the time there is. There is not any more. There are sixty minutes in an hour, twenty-four hours in a day, and seven days in a week. There are many people that accomplish great deeds within this time. How did Ben Franklin spend his day in order to develop so many skills? How did Thomas Edison have the time to discover so many inventions? How do the top executives in business find a period of rest and relaxation while running multi-billion dollar companies? How does the working woman with primary childcare responsibilities fit it all in? Within each hour, day, and week, is an abundance of time to accomplish our goals. How we use our time will dictate how far we travel toward our goals before our batteries run out. It also affects how happy we are during the journey.

The first lesson of time management is to identify where our time currently goes. "Like sand in an hourglass, so go the days of our lives," says the opening credits of a television soap opera. What are we spending our time doing while the sand goes down the drain? Is it what we should be doing to advance our purpose and goals?

The best time management technique that I have found to identify where I spend the minutes of my hours is by using a "time log" for a couple of weeks. You may have heard of techniques that tell you to write down what you are doing every fifteen minutes to discover what you are working on and for how long. In my opinion, that does not go far enough to catalog the wasted minutes that rapidly add up to hours, and eventually to days and weeks.

OPPORTUNITY:

Try this technique instead. For the next week—or two weeks if you are really determined to find an accurate study of your time—write down <u>everything</u> you are doing, right down to the minute. This may seem overly burdensome, but it will be quite revealing. If you spend 3:02 p.m. to 3:06 p.m. writing a business memo, write it down. If your phone rings at 3:06 p.m. and you talk until 3:09, write it down. If you spend 3:09 p.m. until 3:16 p.m. talking to a colleague who stops by your office, write it down. Photocopy the following log to give you plenty of room to record. After a week during which you are studying your time habits, tally up the total time you spend doing each task during the business day. Record your personal time as well.

Time Log Study

<u>Actual Time</u>	<u>Activity</u>	<u>Length of time on activity</u>
Example:		
8:00 a.m.	Arrived at office, read newspaper	11 minutes
8:11 a.m.	Checked emails	4 minute
8:15 a.m.	Talked to coworker	12 minutes

Etc. Now conduct your own time study:

Time Log Study

<u>Actual Time</u>   <u>Activity</u>   <u>Length of time on activity</u>

After completion of the study, objectively analyze the results. If you are the typical person, it will shock you. You may think that you spent one and a half hours working on that report your boss wants next Tuesday, but when you pull out the interruptions, daydreaming, and other tasks you squeezed in, you may find you have spent only half that time actually working on the project.

Daily Time Log Summary

<u>Activity</u>	<u>Total Average</u> <u>Day Time</u>	<u>Percentage of</u> <u>day</u>
Preparing and eating meals		
Important relationships		
Personal time (showering, etc.)		
Important phone calls/meetings		
Unimportant interruptions		
Planning		
Non-goal-oriented conversation		
Daydreaming		
Watching TV		
Family time		
Reading		
Working on my business goals		
Other		

What is the value of such a time study? There are lots of books on the market that can help us become more organized and use our time wisely, and I think all of us can continually use our time more efficiently and effectively. But the detailed study of our own time habits should be so astonishing, it will jolt us into how we view our work and personal day.

When we look at the results of our study we may find that 20 percent of our day is taken up by watching television, 10 percent is consumed by non-goal-oriented conversation, 10 percent used up by unimportant interruptions, and 10 percent involves daydreaming or frustrated inactivity. These alone could take up 50 percent of our productive day. What if we could use at least half that time for important planning, goal-setting, and focusing on goal-oriented activity? Ask yourself "Lakein's Question" to figure how you should spend your time. Time management consultant Alan Lakein suggests that we ask ourselves, *"What is the best use of my time right now?"*[68] By asking this question of ourselves frequently we will automatically refocus our efforts on what we deem as truly important.

Many of us spend each day casually consuming the time God gave us here on earth. It does not mean that we are intentionally wasting our time, but many of us do not realize the value of it. Ben Franklin said, "Time is money." And since we can *all* relate to money, here is one way how we can recognize the value of our time.

OPPORTUNITY:

Once you have the time log results, try another calculation. Determine how much money per hour your employer pays you for your time. Or better yet, since most of us feel we are not reimbursed for our true value, come up with a figure that you think your time is worth. Don't be bashful. Put a generous figure on what you deserve. Then, multiply your dollar figure by each category of time spent according to your time log. For example, if you have determined that your time is actually worth $50 an hour, including benefits, and you spent an average of thirty minutes a day shooting the breeze with your coworkers instead of actually working, you can place a weekly value of that activity at $50 X .5 hour a day = $25 per day.

How Much My Time is Worth

$_____ *per hour.*

$_____ *how much I invested in activities that could have been applied to my goals.*

Now, let's switch gears. Imagine that we are the employer who pays our employees $50 an hour plus benefits. We can do this because we are the "boss" of our own activities. We run our own personal company—our life. Now, speaking as an employer, would we give $25 a day to someone whose job it is to babble to a coworker about something they saw on TV last night? I should think not. If we would not tolerate this as an employer, why do we tolerate it with ourselves? If we place a high enough value on our time, we will recognize that each hour is precious and we will be reluctant to squander minutes of it doing unimportant activity.

This is not to say that we should not talk to coworkers or even not "zone-out" during the workday to relax our mind. We need to be sociable and must rest every hour from our jobs that require our top concentration. However, the results of our time log may show that it is not the dessert we consume after our daily meals that fattens us up and slows our progress, it is the excessive in-between-meal snacking of time items that has little to do with our goals.

I always thought I had respectable work habits, but after conducting this time log for the first time, I was amazed at the idle time I spent shooting the bull with coworkers, fidgeting at my desk, concentrating on non-work related activities, or passing time with trivial and frivolous subjects. The stun I received by this revelation commanded my attention, and I immediately changed my work methods to make better use of my time. The trauma alone of discovering where our time is gradually sucked away by the hourglass is enough to convince us to make better use of "all the time there is."

Once we have identified our "time wasters," it is then up to us to *prioritize* our time. The well-known story of how public relations expert Ivy Lee helped steel executive Charles Schaub is a good example of prioritization and efficiency. The tale began when Charles Schaub, president of US Steel in the 1920s, sought to improve efficiency in his management. Schaub felt that his company was a good one, but it could be better. He called in Lee to help out. Lee instructed Schaub and his managers to make a daily list of items to be accomplished during the business day, and then rank them in order of importance. Then, Lee said, "do them." Lee said the managers should work on the most important task first until it was finished, before moving on to the next item. Lee did not ask for immediate compensation for his overly simple advice, he simply told Schaub to try out the new system for a few months and then send him a check for what he thought the advice was worth. After a few months of using "prioritization," the results were so effective, Schaub sent Lee a check for $25,000.[69] That was a lot of money back then for Lee's "paragraph" of advice. After applying prioritization in my own life and seeing the results, I now feel that Lee was seriously *underpaid*.

To make prioritization more effective, obtain a good daily planner system. We can even develop one of our own. It does not really matter what we use, as long as we follow Ivy Lee's advice. We need to write down the daily objectives we want to accomplish and prioritize them. You could use the classic, A, B & C codes:

- *A* items are those that we *must* do to forward toward our goals.

- *B* items are those that we should do, but are not an immediate priority.

- *C* items are those that may be nice to do, but are not absolutely necessary today.

Next, prioritize the items by numbering them (A-1, A-2, A-3, B-1, B-2, etc.). We need to work on the A-1 item first. *Then* only move on to the A-2 when A-1 is completed or we have exhausted our maximum effectiveness on the item. We do not go to the B's until we finish with the A's unless we determine our energy would be better spent there for a while.

Handheld computer organizers are fine, but remember, our goals must always be staring us in the face if we want our subconscious minds to be working on them behind the scenes. Our time is the most precious valuable we possess and quality use of it is critical. With a daily planner system, we can outline our short-term, intermediate-term, and long-term goals and assign regular resources to dedicate to pursue those objectives. Blocking out time in writing compels us to act on the time we assigned each day. A planner system is useful for our personal time as well. Our weekend "to do" lists become "will act" lists when we schedule a block of time to accomplish them in proper priority. Use of a priority time-planner system will not guarantee that we will accomplish every objective on our list. But it will ensure that we spend our priceless time on the most important goals we have.

Remember that efficiency is not necessarily effectiveness. Let's make sure we concentrate on tasks that are important and effective in reaching our objectives such as planning, self-improvement, and nourishing our relationships, and not time-wasters such as television, needless business meetings, and idle discussions. For example, many business and success books talk of the four categories of time use, including:

- *urgent, important* items like life-and-death emergencies that demand your time;

- *urgent, but not important* tasks such as endless phone calls, pointless meetings, or others who tell us their needs should be important to us;

- *not urgent, not important* tasks such as aimless Internet surfing or television viewing of shows we really are not interested in; and finally,

- *not urgent, but important* tasks such as spending time on vital relationships, self-improvement activities, goal-setting, and achievement.

Obviously, the last category is where we should schedule most of our time.

In their book *Managing Your Mind*, Gillian Butler and Tony Hope state that the central principle of time management is "spend your time doing those things you value or that help you achieve your goals."[70] By deciding which of our activities is *important, but not necessarily urgent,* we can devote our time accordingly.

OPPORTUNITY:

List three <u>un</u>important activities you can either reduce or eliminate and what important activities you can substitute instead.

1.

2.

3.

P) *Physiology*

To every action there is always opposed an equal reaction.—Sir Isaac Newton

How do we *feel* depressed? That is, not are we depressed, or what makes us feel depressed. But if we wanted to feel depressed right now, how would we move our body? Would we hold our head up high, smile brightly, and give a little whistle? Or would we sit down, head hung low, and groan? Wait, we say, once we feel depressed, then our body responds with a depressed posture. Conversely, when we feel happy, we smile and look positive. Maybe so, but is this a chicken-and-egg question? Can the opposite be true?

Physiology is the science dealing with the functions of living organisms. Another way to define this in human terms is the science of how we move our body. Have you ever tried to feel depressed when you walked down the street while whistling and doing jumping jacks? Try it, if you dare. It is real hard. What do we tell our children when they get a cut or scrape or experience a childhood disappointment? "Chin up!" we tell them.

How we move our body can have a definite impact on our emotions. Many doctors advise their patients to begin exercise programs not only because of the health gains, but also due to the positive emotional benefits of vigorous physical activities. Whenever I have a problem to be solved, I spend time thinking about it while on the running track at the health club. The "endorphins" released by my body lead me to clearer thinking, and I often figure out a solution to the problem where I was simply at a roadblock at my office desk. Activity helps me to form a positive outlook to effectively find the proper route to my goals. If we are looking to change our emotions and our thinking, let's begin by changing our posture, our activity, and even our facial expressions. Remember the *Goal Motivation Wheel*? Start with physical action, and the positive *feelings* will follow. Hold your head up and give a little whistle!

Q) *Quietness*

A closed mouth gathers no feet.—Anonymous

Throughout this book, I have referred to a lot of action, planning, and accomplishing of goals. However, there also must be time for reflection and contemplation. We must regularly give enough attention to being quiet, as well as making noise by taking action. For every day, there is a night. Even God rested for a day after creating the heavens and the earth. Therefore, that was a signal that we must rest and review our progress, give thanks for what we have received and accomplished, recharge our batteries, and ask for guidance in our next activity.

It is difficult in today's stressful world to unload our daily burdens. But meditation and prayer are two ways that can help. For example, as author Jon Kabat-Zinn explains, as opposed to ruminating over all of the clutter in our brains, mediation is the process of emptying our muddled thoughts to increase our mindfulness.[71] Recent research suggests that those who incorporate meditation training in their stressful lives reported improved moods, feeling engaged again in their work, increased energy, and less anxiety.[72] Likewise, prayer is a time-tested practice that brings comfort to the afflicted.

I believe the reason prayer and meditation are so effective for so many of us is because we finally are quiet enough to listen to the answers provided by God through our own consciousness. In prayer, the solutions to our predicaments are turned over to God to solve. As we reflect, we get the answers we requested. Meditation can remove negative thoughts that can dominate our thinking. When we engage in these methods, our intuition takes over and provides many of the revelations we seek.

R) *Risk*

It was a risk I had to take—and took.—Robert Frost

One of the steps on the famous psychologist Abraham Maslow's "hierarchy of needs" is *security*. All of us desire to be secure and be insulated from problems and stress. But what it means to be alive in this world is for us to face our daily problems and challenges. To overcome them, we must be courageous enough to take some chances. The only way to grow is to be like a seed—sprout and push ourselves out of our comfort zone from the protective earth and into the wild. There is a risk of being stepped on while we are just seedlings, but without taking a risk, we will never have the opportunity to flower.

Risk. We face it every day. And many of us try to avoid it. But nothing worth reaching in this world is actually attained without some element of risk. We are not talking about gambling and freely engaging in life-or-death precipitous ventures. But we must be ready to accept "educated risks"—the chances we take and the choices we make in everyday living. The only truly secure person is the one in the graveyard.

OPPORTUNITY:

Name one "educated" risk you have not taken until now.

S) *Service*

Whoever wishes to be great among you must be your servant, and whoever wishes to be first among you must be slave of all.—Jesus Christ

At one time or another, we all have felt like we deserved a raise. "I'm doing everything I'm expected to do around here and I've haven't received a promotion in a long time," we complain to a coworker. Well, if we are doing what is expected, isn't that what we were hired for in the first place at a salary we agreed upon when we signed on with our employer? Why in the world would someone pay us more than what was bargained if we are *only* doing the job that is expected?

If we want to receive a larger paycheck, we have to do *more* than what we are paid to do. After a while, we will discover one of two things. First, our employer may realize how valuable we are and raise our compensation to keep us from leaving their organization to the competition. Seem far-fetched? If we do not receive a higher salary for exceeding our expectations, we may recognize that it is time to move on to another company, or perhaps, another career. The choice is ours. But, at the very least, we have little room to gripe about our earnings when it is our option to work harder and provide a higher level of needed service, or move on to where our service is better appreciated.

Motivational guru Zig Ziglar says, you can get anything you want in life, if you "help enough other people get what they want."[73] If our traditional corporate customer—our employer—is not recognizing the benefits from our service, we may want to strike out on our own, either launching a side business or even staking our own claim in the business world. Futurist Faith Popcorn's book *Clicking* depicts future trends for the American work force. Popcorn says that working on our own is the trend for more and more people, especially women. "How many countless times over the years have you heard the refrain of a woman in a traditional corporate job complain 'there's got to be a better way.' No the lament is more action-oriented, crooning, 'I'll do it my way.' And that way for more than 7.7 million women is to start their own businesses."[74]

A second component of service is aiding others who need our help. As we age, the urge to make a contribution to our society both in financial and human terms grows. But many of us are reluctant to take action by ourselves. If we are not the outgoing type, volunteering at the abused family center or our local agency for the blind may be a bit intimidating. Here's one way to contribute without being bold. Join a service club. There are thousands of service clubs in the United States and throughout the world that benefit others who need assistance. It does not matter whether we participate in the Kiwanis, Rotary, Zonta, Jaycees, Junior League, or our own church group. Or we can call our local United Way if we do not have a particular cause in mind. They can direct us to an active volunteer program at many needy nonprofit agencies. There is security and safety in numbers. We will discover that it is a lot more fun volunteering our service hours elbow-to-elbow with others of similar backgrounds and experiences than venturing out on our own. But no matter how we decide to give our time and dollar donations to those organizations and people who need a helping hand, we will enrich our own lives by serving them.

Albert Einstein was once questioned on what the meaning of life was. Without hesitation he replied, "To serve others, of course." Jesus repeatedly said his purpose on earth was to serve others. He proved that the greatest leaders are also the greatest servants. If we serve our employees, our staffs, our families, our children, our neighbors, and especially, those who have the least, we will become the greatest leaders we can possibly be.

OPPORTUNITY:

Name one act of service you will commit to in the next year (e.g., join a service club, volunteer at a food bank, help a literacy group, etc.).

T) *Toughness*

Never give in. Never give in. Never, never, never, never...—Winston Churchill

Toughness, tenacity, persistence, intestinal fortitude...in other words, guts. Whatever you want to call it, maximum goal-achievers have it. Most rookie professional sports athletes do not score the first time they put their hands on the ball, shoot toward the basket, or swing a bat. Those that do succeed have an extensive legacy of failure behind them. The geniuses in the world who have succeeded more than anyone else have also failed more than anyone else has. The great inventor Thomas Edison discovered so many new inventions not only because he was brilliant, but also he attempted more experiments than anyone else did. The living legend in professional basketball Michael Jordan lead his team in scoring not only due to his talent and hard practice, but because he took more shots! Many of the greatest home-run hitters in baseball also lead the record books in strikeouts. These heroes were tough and tenacious. Who are some of this nation's greatest presidents in terms of persistence? Abraham Lincoln's long list of lost elections, Franklin Delano Roosevelt's struggle with polio, or Harry Truman's failure in business did not stop those goal-achievers from meeting the biggest challenges America faced. When asked to give a commencement address at his childhood school, British Prime Minister Winston Churchill rose to the podium and said, "Never give in. Never give in. Never, never, never, never—in nothing great or small, large or petty, never give in except to convictions of honor and good sense," and then he sat down. Though it may have been the shortest commencement address ever given, he made his point. Toughness and tenacity pay off when we have the right purpose. In his famous "We will fight" speech, Churchill told the bombed-out English people during times of horrendous defeats for the British armed forces that they would fight "in the hills and in the streets. We shall never surrender." After the comment, Churchill allegedly covered the microphone and said they would hit the

Germans over the head with a beer bottle, because that's about all they had to fight with. Despite the overwhelming odds, Britain prevailed. But it could not have done so without incredible "toughness."

In our own lives, let's make the commitment to our goals to do whatever it takes to achieve, as long as it is in line with the correct principles outlined in our purpose statement. We often get frustrated after repeated attempts to reach our goal if we do not experience success fast enough or if we cannot seem to master our chosen skill after several attempts. Remember that practice does NOT make *perfect*. Perfection is analogous to *infinity*. Practice makes *improvement*. If we notice our results and change our tactics to conform to changing circumstances, we will notice improvements. The Japanese principle of "Kaisen," (constant and never-ending improvement) will soon see that we are indeed *approaching infinity*.

U) *Union*

We must all hang together, or assuredly, we shall all hang separately.
—Benjamin Franklin

Two heads are better than one.

That simple axiom is what is behind the concept of *union*. No person is successful in this world without the help of others. We use other people's knowledge, coaching, guidance, experience, assistance, and money to get ahead. And so we should. Since the beginning of time, man has been a social creature, first using the experience and aid of other members of his/her clan to hunt the hairy mammoth and build a fire. The most successful individuals in the world today, whether they are a contented retiree or a multi-millionaire movie star, utilized the help of others to climb up the ladder of prosperity.

How can we use the concept of *union* to assist us to reach our goals? One example occurred during the Great Depression. When President Franklin Delano Roosevelt took office, he, of course, had a cabinet of secretaries. But what Roosevelt also formed became known as the "Kitchen Cabinet." This was a group of experts in various areas that Roosevelt consulted to help find solutions to the great problems of America's broken economy. Though not appointed officials, their expertise helped Roosevelt develop the New Deal that eventually assisted in the country's effort to address the horrible economic problems of the day.

Napoleon Hill interviewed dozens of successful achievers in his day. What he found in many cases was that these great goal-setters often used the brains of others to accomplish their objectives. Hill called this strategy the "Master Mind Principle." That is, two or more people working in positive harmony to attain a specific objective.[75] In today's corporate lingo, we call this the "team." Many progressive corporations have found that teams, or "quality circles," can find solutions to sticky problems in today's competitive marketplace. Countless research studies show that groups make better decisions than individuals on their own. A team, managed and led well by an empowering leader, can produce better results than a "boss" can map out in the executive suite all by him or herself. Team building is now vogue in many companies that realize that many brains contributing to a common goal are much better than one. We can apply this "Master Mind Principle" in our own lives.

OPPORTUNITY:

What people would you like to put on your "Kitchen Cabinet?" They can be someone we know, or like our models, someone that we have never met. Collaborate with other "geniuses" to inspire you forward. Remember the analogy as your life as a corporation. Who would you appoint to your "Board of Directors" to provide expert advice and sagacious guidance to your next step toward your goals. You should not rely on a single "mentor" to guide you. That person may have a specific agenda and you may just be a cog in their wheel that turns in alignment to their own goals. If you have a group of mentors, you can benefit by the advice of those who may have different opinions on how to achieve a certain task. By appointing your own "Kitchen Cabinet," you can possess many times the resources than you would own on your own. List the top five members of your "Kitchen Cabinet."

In our journey toward our goals, we will have many mentors, but chances are, we too will become beacons of guiding light for others. It has been said that no man or woman is a permanent success without taking others along with them. We are also reminded that it is "lonely at the top." And that will be true if we do not participate in the lives of others that will obviously seek our counseling once we become a top goal-achiever. As we become more powerful, the "law of attraction" will draw other similar persons to us. We can play a significant role in their plans, as well as absorb useful lessons by the trials and tribulations of others.

To achieve consistent success toward our goals, we must accept that no one is an island unto himself or herself. Like a flock of geese, we must often travel in a "V-formation" that uses all of the group's talents that eventually benefit everyone. Sometimes, we are the leaders, pointing in the direction of our desired destination, taking on the head wind all by ourselves. But, also like geese, we must know when to break off from the front and let someone else take the primary position and drop back when we are tired, using the benefit of drafting off others. Competitive team bikers and marathon runners do this. All great leaders were at one time great followers. Although we may not idealize the comparison of our lofty human pursuits to a flock of geese flying south for the winter, we cannot deny that these birds travel a long, laborious journey to get to where they want to go. And, despite the arduous trek in the face of stiff winds, they get there.

V) *Vocabulary*

It is so plain to me that eloquence, like swimming, is an art which all men might learn, though so few do.—Ralph Waldo Emerson

In today's business world, no skill is touted as having more importance as the ability to communicate effectively. Whether it is legible and understandable written skills, interpersonal communication ability, or the eloquent talent of vocal and body language dexterity in delivering a sales presentation, the personal power that helps individuals move ahead is not built by raw talent in their area of expertise alone. The ability to communicate effectively is a required ticket to today's game of life. Often, excellent written and verbal skills are not only desired by today's business leaders, it is mandated.

We must not only be competent writers and speakers to our coworkers, our customers, our vendors, and our supervisors, we must also be superior communicators with ourselves. This personal "self-talk" helps define how to express our feelings to others. Do we use emotionally charged power words in a positive tone in our own self-talk? Or do we feed dull and apathetic thoughts into our mind. Because we are creatures with a verbal-oriented language, we naturally talk to ourselves constantly in the same voice. Our use of language is the primary key to unveil our desired thoughts.

For example, when we open our eyes in the morning for the first time, what are the first thoughts that pop into our mind? Do we say to ourselves: "Great! Another fantastic day that I am alive. I am so thankful for all the pleasurable things I have in my life and I am extremely excited that I get another chance to live a life in a free nation where I can pursue my goals and desires!"?

Or, do we say: "Oh, no, not another day. I'm so tired, and I can't believe I have to get up and go to work—again! And that project that is waiting for me, who needs it? My eyelids feel like they are made of lead. Where's the coffee?"

It may seem Pollyanna to greet each morning with a smile and a whistle, but conversely, what sense does it make to salute the day with a frown and a groan? Each attitude we adopt is one we purposely select from our cafeteria of emotions. Our personal outlook is our responsibility, and our attitude is within our control. Why eat canned prunes when we can have fresh fruit off the vine!

When we go through our day and use our virtually unlimited vocabulary to describe our feelings and experiences, let's try removing words like "I hate, I'll try, and I should." Replace them with "I prefer and I will." Similarly, let's soften negative words that are in our vocabulary. Let's not be "confused" by the perplexing problem at work. Instead, let's be "curious," and we will approach the situation with a positive, creative problem-solving attitude. Likewise, we need to energize positive words we use. Let's not just be strong; let's be "invincible!"

The power of our communication with others is not only in what we say, but also in what we don't say. Remember the timely advice: "God gave us two ears and one mouth to listen twice as much as we talk." It is true that we learn absolutely nothing when we speak, but we can discover infinitesimal amounts by listening to others. Those individuals who spend more time listening to others are held in higher regard than those who are constantly blowing their own horn. It is true. Take it from me, a constant horn blower!

Steven Covey lists as one of his *Seven Habits of Highly Effective People,* "Seek first to understand, then to be understood."[76] The value of our communication is not totally dependent on what we say. More important to those who we communicate with is how to listen to them. How many times has a close friend come to us with a problem or crisis in their life, and not let us get a word in edgewise? But by using empathic listening, after the monologue of woes, our friend thanks us profusely for talking with them. And we hardly said a word. Obviously, listening is much more powerful than talking.

Try this. The next time you meet with a friend or attend a meeting or function, try to concentrate on saying as *little* as possible. You should maintain eye contact with others in the room, and give a sign of listening by nodding your head, even if you have a different opinion. This does not mean that you agree, but only that you acknowledge their opinion. If you have an incredible urge to say, "What I think..." bite your tongue. Instead, ask others, "What do you think?"

If you have communication apprehension (i.e., you are on the shy side), you can still be involved in active communication by making sure others know you are listening. If you are totally quiet, your partners in communication may think you are bored or are not listening. Though you may not want to say much, respond in some way, physically or verbally, with others in the room. Say, "Is that so?" or "Tell me more."

When we practice active listening instead of launching into a soliloquy to please our own egos, those around us will suddenly consider us "great communicators."

W) *Wonder*

Anyone who keeps learning stays young.—Henry Ford

Did we stop asking questions about the world when we became an adult? At what age did we stop asking others, "Tell me why?" At what point did we consciously decide that we had learned enough about the world and had seen everything under the sun? Have we ever taken an adult education class and seen several senior citizens learning new skills such as computer training? What's the point, we may wonder? My goodness, if we are pushing seventy, why bother to learn anything new?

The ancients taught us: "Life is a continuous river in motion." If we do not move forward in the current, we do not remain in one place. Instead, we are swept backward. It takes effort just to tread water in the ever-moving stream of today's society. Without learning to swim, we may find this dip in a running brook may eventually send us over mighty waterfalls. We have seen examples of companies, social movements, or individuals that persist in a state of non-growth. Soon they fade away and are swept over the falls of a swiftly flowing world. If our minds are the greatest computer machines ever created, the lack of new and improving input will certainly rust them quickly.

The longer we live, we realize that the concept of perpetual learning, or endless *wonder*, adds quality to our years. What's the point of continual study if we are in a late stage of life? On the other hand, what's the point of life at any age if we are not consistently improving ourselves? What value is there to assiduous learning? Efficiency-trainer Brian Tracy and learning-expert Colin Rose in their book *Accelerated Learning Techniques* claim you can learn anything you want—the key is to knowing how to learn by adopting the right state of mind, understanding your own learning style, and always asking questions.[77] If our aspiration is to serve others, our ever-present sense of wonder will make us better servants. If our purpose is to teach our children, our example of seeking expanded knowledge and insight will both inspire and augment their learning. If our plan is to build a better mousetrap, we cannot go forward without an increased capability to absorb new concepts. Let's keep a "childlike" wonder present in our lives, absorbing new knowledge, understanding, and viewpoints like a dry sponge.

X) Xylophone

Last night I shot an elephant in my pajamas. How he got into my pajamas, I don't know.—Groucho Marx

X obviously represents Xylophone. No human being should go through life without learning how to play the *xylophone*. Am I serious? Of course not! But that is what we need to accept. We need *non-seriousness* in our lives. And a xylophone is an instrument that certainly can make us laugh. A good dose of humor (even weak humor!) will cure a lot of ills as we sometimes stumble up the bumpy path to our goals.

We must laugh at our mistakes, not groan at our misfortunes. We must not take ourselves too seriously. A recent survey revealed that the average person laughs about twelve to twenty times a day. We should increase that ten-fold. Our goals are important, but everything needs to be pursued with a grain of fun. Often, much of our life needs an entire silo of amusement! How else could we get through the many challenges we face? It is a lot easier to continue to wear a warm smile when our attitudes are sublime. But when small disappointments are made out to be natural disasters, a poor temperament can impede our progress. When we can make light of our petty "problems," they are less likely to lead to discouragement. Or as Mother Teresa of Calcutta once stated, *laughter is a cure for misery.*

After losing in a landslide in his quest for the White House in 1984, former Vice President Walter Mondale told reporters the day after his massive defeat, "I always wanted to run for president in the worst possible way. And I did." After being shot by an attempted assassin in 1981, President Ronald Reagan told the doctors in the emergency room, "I hope you are all Republicans!" Can we laugh in the face of defeat and disappointment?

There are very few of us who will lose a crushing presidential defeat like Mondale or experience a life-and-death situation like Reagan. But imagine facing such incredible disappointment or crisis with such aplomb and grace. Is it any wonder why leaders like Reagan and Mondale rose to the top of their respective political parties? They were goal-setters who still managed to keep life in perspective. The next time you face a serious challenge on the way to your goals, think of the xylophone and smile.

Y) *Youthful*

I think I don't regret a single "excess" of my responsive youth—I only regret, in my chilled age, certain occasions and possibilities I didn't embrace.—Henry James

"Why don't you grow up!"

To paraphrase Peter Pan, what's the point of growing up? Those people who seem to be having the most fun in life also seem to be the most youthful, despite any age. Besides having more energy than most other people have, those with a young mind-set also seem to be more pleasant, happier, and healthier than many other persons their "age." They laugh more and do not take themselves too seriously. They see life as one big playground and jump from the swing set to the merry-go-round with a single bound. In fact, often times they act just like children! Imagine that, grown-ups pretending they are a bunch of kids at the amusement park!

Do we have a seemingly unlimited amount of energy stored in a secret compartment? Do we find fascination in the simplest things? Those who have a *youthful* attitude are not prejudicial, cynical, or gloomy. Those negative dispositions are learned attitudes from "adults." Most children possess awe about life. They exude an air of limitless possibilities about achieving goals. Children, unlike us "experienced and educated" adults, do not know very much. They have not been told enough times that "you can't do that," or "it's not possible." Is it any wonder that children have such great imaginations and optimistic hopes about life? Imagine if we can recapture that youthful attitude. Though children do have bouts of selfishness from time to time, generally, they are less possessive and are among the most generous creatures on earth. Don't we wish we could always act like that?

Those who pooh-pooh having a *youthful* attitude may seem like they are acting responsible and mature, but in reality, they may be insecure and depressed. Does that mean that youthful people are irresponsible? Of course not. Those who are in control of their lives are always responsible, they just do not get upset about the "small stuff" in life.

A friend of mine knows that we do not give up having childlike dreams easily. She finished her first marathon after running twenty-six miles in fifty-degree weather. On the day of the race, she was sixty-one years old. A decade later, she is still competing. More than four years after leaving the White House, President George Herbert Walker Bush could have spent the rest of his life in a rocking chair, pondering his memoirs. Instead, the sixty-nine-year-old former leader of the free world parachuted out of an airplane, the same way he did at age nineteen when his plane was shot down over the Pacific Ocean during World War II. We have heard and read the reports of grandmothers soaring down a raging river white-water rafting or going back to college to earn a degree. True, our bodies do give out on us, eventually. But more often than not, our minds do not have to stop a youthful attitude due to age. On the contrary, we often intentionally turn our minds off by ceasing to learn new ideas, refusing to express a sense of humor, or preventing ourselves from rebounding once we face a temporary defeat. Imagine a child quitting the effort to walk after the first time they stumbled and fell on their behind.

How do we stay youthful? Like most points mentioned in this book, it is all a state of mind. We must stay curious. That way we will always seek another route to our goal if one particular path is roadblocked. Let's continue to feed new material into our minds. If we want to be young, we must act young. Move like a child. Smile like a child. Laugh like a child. Think like a child. Give like a child. We are all God's children, are we not? It is about time we started acting like one.

Z) *Zone*

If you refuse to accept anything but the best, you very often get it.
—W. Somerset Maugham

When a basketball player is hitting every shot he or she puts up, they are said to be *in the zone*. How do we learn to operate within our "*zone?*" First, we must be ready for our lessons when they are presented to us. That brings us to another Z word—Zen. There is a Zen saying that states, "When the student is ready, the teacher will appear." If goal achievement is due to a strict adherence to a relatively simple set of principles, why aren't more people accomplishing a level of success that brings them full satisfaction? One might postulate that if this time-tested information is given to everyone on earth, we would wipe out world hunger, end all wars, and provide prosperity to all. I believe it could. But it will not.

Why?

Basically, because the five percent of individuals who consciously choose a noble purpose, form written goals for their life, and spend time improving their minds and bodies are the same five percent who rise as the cream of the crop in their chosen endeavors. The other 95 percent are not ready to learn. However, for those that are, slowly, but surely, the teachers, role models, and mentors of success will appear out of nowhere. Successful people create a readiness for learning, and like a sponge, soak up the lessons of true mastery. Once we achieve our adroitness, our prosperity will be measured by our contribution to the needs of others, which will, in turn, enrich our own souls.

In order to get *in the zone*, we have to exercise all of the practices we have discussed in this book to the best of our ability. Who is *in the zone*? They are the ones who will:

- Exhibit a positive *attitude*;
- Possess a *belief* in their dreams;
- Have *consistency* in their efforts;
- Thirst in their *desire* for their goals;
- Drink the nourishment of *energy* to fuel their efforts;
- View their goals in *focus*;
- Have written *goals* with attached victory dates;
- Create *habits* that reflect the practice of success;
- *Image positively*, rehearsing their future victories;
- Enjoy the *journey* that life provides;
- Research and seek increasing *knowledge* to accomplish their dreams;

- Feel *love* for themselves and for others;

- *Model* excellence whenever they see it;

- Accept *no excuses*, but rather, alter their methods in face of trials, and try again;

- Establish *organization* in their lives and manage time wisely;

- Use active *physiology* to create vibrant energy and positive attitudes;

- Ponder during periods of *quietness*, give thanks to God, and ask for guidance;

- Accept *risk* as a part of being alive, realizing nothing is worth achieving without taking a chance;

- Fulfill the need for providing *service* to others;

- Show a *toughness* to overcome obstacles;

- Cast a *union* with other like minds to increase the possibility of fruition;

- Use a positive, powerful *vocabulary* to increase the effectiveness of their communication and listen to others;

- Maintain a sense of *wonder* about the ever-increasing marvels in the world;

- Never fail to keep a sense of humor, even if it takes learning how to play the *xylophone!*; and

- Manifest a childlike sentiment of *youthful* enthusiasm.

Those who can employ those characteristics are goal-winners, purpose achievers, and personally powerful. They are operating *IN THE ZONE.*

Epilogue

Life is a daring adventure, or it is nothing.—Helen Keller

If a blind, deaf, and dumb girl who, with the aid of a wonderful teacher, blossomed into a great intellectual and found life daring, why can't we? Have we been blind to our innermost dreams? Have we been deaf to our calling to accomplish the great tasks that only we can attain? Have we been dumb to the skills and effort it takes to excel in our purpose in life? The teachers are all around us. Those teachers are called life. Are we prepared to learn from the lessons? Are we willing to study harder even when life doles out a failing grade on a crucial test?

In April 1997, twenty-one-year-old golfer Tiger Woods smashed numerous records in the Masters Golf Tournament in Augusta, Georgia. He was the youngest person and the first African-American or Asian-American to win the prestigious match, and he beat the competition by the largest margin ever with the lowest score in the hundred-year history of the four-day-long tournament. Coincidentally, Wood's achievement in his first major tournament as a professional, came fifty years to the week that baseball legend Jackie Robinson broke the color barrier and became the first African-American to play in segregated Major League baseball in the United States. Wood's victory, and other similar breakthroughs, will hopefully produce a generation of dream-filled children, who will see that anything is possible in this great country of ours if we set a worthy purpose with challenging goals, desire them intensely, and effectively work toward them. Whether our dream is to be a top PGA golfer, or to be the best parent we can be, we can realize that dream with a resolute grip of belief in the skills that God granted us. Tiger Woods said himself, "I hope I can influence kids in a positive way."[78] All of us should have the same feeling.

Like the three little pigs who hoped to live a long, satisfying, and worthwhile life while avoiding the big, bad wolf, we have chosen where we wanted to build our house of goals by selecting a sturdy foundation, or sense of purpose. That aim not only improves the quality of our own life, but also makes a substantial contribution to the lives of others. We then took a walk and surveyed the different materials to build our home. We then selected the values we hold most important and the positive beliefs of faith that we either reinforced or made an effort to change to make our home strong, safe, and secure. Next, we designed our own blueprint of destiny by forming worthy goals that were aligned with our stated purpose and in accord with our values. Finally, as we started to take that first step toward our destination, we studied the essential skills and knowledge necessary to make our journey a fulfilling one.

Rome, the saying states, was not built in a day. And neither will our goals be achieved in one single move. But every small worthy action accomplished each day will string together an exemplary life each and every one of us deserves to live.

There is a lovely story told by Rabbi Harold Kushner in his book, *When All You Ever Wanted Isn't Enough*, about the managers of a factory, who suspected that an employee was stealing company property. Each day, the employee would exit the factory pushing a wheelbarrow full of garbage. The managers hired a security guard to search through the garbage in an effort to find out what that employee was stealing. Every day for two weeks the security guard searched for elusive stolen articles through the disgusting array of rubbish. Finally, the security guard gave up. He stopped the employee and said, "I know you are stealing something, but I don't know what it is. It is driving me crazy and I won't look through any more refuse. I'll make a deal with you. If you tell me what you are stealing, I promise not to tell the management."

The employee thought for a moment, and figured he had nothing to lose at that point and said to the security guard, "I'm stealing wheelbarrows."[79]

The moral of the story is that we spend so much time searching through the garbage in our own lives—the misfortune, the disasters, the fears, the hatred, the resentment, the negative attitudes, etc.—in a vain attempt to find meaning and happiness. We often forget that the gift granted to us by God—our beautiful reward—is the gift of life itself. What we do with that gift is up to us.

In your journey of goal-setting and achievement, fill your "wheelbarrow" full of joy, of love of service, and of accomplishments brimming with the best that you can offer the world. God bless you and I hope you and I can meet someday on the road as we are *Approaching Infinity!*

Approaching Infinity
Six-Step Goal-Setting Action Plan

1. Statement of goal:

2. List three reasons why you want to achieve it:

-
-
-

3. List challenges to overcome:

4. Who can help you?

5. What skills and knowledge are necessary?

6. Immediate Action Plan:

-
-
-
-

Endnotes

1. Nichols, Ralph G. and Leonard Stevens. "Listening to People," *Harvard Business Review* 35 (1957), 85–92.

2. Nightingale, Earl. "The Strangest Secret Revisited," *Earl Nightingale's Greatest Discovery* (New York: Dodd, Mead & Company, 1987).

3. King, Larry. *How to Talk to Anyone, Anytime, Anywhere: The Secrets of Good Communication* (New York: Random House, 1994), 194.

4. Science, 2003, *National Public Radio*, February 7, 2003.

5. Burns, George. *100 Years, 100 Stories* (New York: G.P. Putnam's Sons, 1997), vii.

6. Fiore, Neil. "Fully Alive After Cancer," *Coping: Living With Cancer* (Franklin, Tennessee: Media America, Inc., January/February 1997).

7. Robbins, Anthony. *Awaken the Giant Within* (New York: Simon and Schuster, 1991), 82.

8. DiFabio, Bill. "A Look Back: No Doubt About Frattare's Love For The Pirates," *Pittsburgh Sports Report*. Retrieved from: http://www.pghsports.com/psr9905/99050101.html.

9. Stanley, Thomas. *The Millionaire Mind* (Kansas City, Missouri: Andrews McMeel, 2000), 34.

10. Allport, G. W. *Pattern and Growth of Personality* (New York: Holt, Reinhart and Winston, 1961).

11. Erikson, T. "Goal-setting and entrepreneurial self-efficacy," *International Journal of Entrepreneurship and Innovation* 3, No. 3, (August, 2002), 183–89.

12. Winfrey, Oprah and Bob Greene. *Making the Connection* (New York: Hyperion, 1996), 32.

13. *The Oxford Dictionary of Word Histories*. Glynnis Chantrell, ed. (Oxford: Oxford University Press, 2002), 137.

14. Blanchard, Ken. *Personal Effectiveness* (New York: Simon and Schuster, 1993).

15. Covey, Steven. *First Things First* (New York: Simon and Schuster, 1994), 51.

16. Covey, Steven. *Principle Centered Leadership* (New York: Summit Books, 1990), 94–100.

17. Maslow, Abraham H. *Toward a Psychology of Being* (Princeton, N.J.: D. Van Nostrand Company, Inc., 1962), 71.

18. Covey. *First Things First*, 44–74.

19. Popcorn, Faith and Lys Marigold. *Clicking: 16 Trends to Future Fit your Life, your Work, and your Business* (New York: Harper Collins Publishers, 1996), 143.

20. Covey, *First Things First*, 59–60.

21. Jones, Laurie Beth. *The Path* (New York: Hyperion, 1996), 3.

22. Verplanken, Bas and Rob W. Holland. "Motivated Decision Making: Effects of Activation and Self-Centrality of Values on Choices and Behavior," *Journal of Personality and Social Psychology* 82, No. 3 (2002), 434–447.

23. Ibid., 434.

24. Hafer, Carolyn L. "Investment in Long-Term Goals and Commitment to Just Means Drive the Need to Believe in a Just World," *Personality and Social Psychology Bulletin* 26, No. 9, (September 2000), 1059–1073.

25. Singer, Stanford. *Journal of Personality and Social Psychology* American Psychological Association, (August 2002).

26. Tracy, Brian. *Pathways to Personal Progress* (Nightingale-Conant, n.d.).

27. Scott, Gini Graham. *The Empowered Mind* (Englewood Cliffs, N.J.: Prentice Hall, 1994).

28. Hill, Napoleon. *Think and Grow Rich* (Greenwich, Conn.: Fawcett Crest, 1937), 70.

29. Josephson, Matthew. *Edison: A Biography* (New York: History Book Club, 1959), 413.

30. Addington, Jack Ensign. *All About Goals and How to Achieve Them* (Marina del Rey, California: DeVorss & Company, 1977), 157.

31. Robbins, 53–72.

32. Freitas, Antonio L., Nira Liberman, Peter Salovey, and Tory E. Higgins. "When to Begin? Regulatory Focus and Initiating Goal Pursuit," *Personality and Social Psychology Bulletin* 28, No. 1, (January 2002).

33. Hafer, 1059–1073.

34. Dawson, Roger. *13 Secrets of Power Performance* (Englewood Cliffs, N.J.: Prentice Hall, 1994), 198–99.

35. King, Laura A. "The Health Benefits of Writing About Life Goals," Southern Methodist University, *Personality and Social Psychology Bulletin* 27 No. 7, (July 2001), 798–807.

36. Waitley, Denis. *The Psychology of Winning* (New York: Simon and Schuster, 1995).

37. Tracy, Brian. *Pathways to Personal Progress* (Nightingale-Conant, n.d.).

38. Jeffries, Susan. *Feel the Fear and Do It Anyway* (San Diego: Harcourt Brace Jovanovich, 1987).

39. Lee, Blaine. *The Power Principle* (New York: Simon and Schuster, 1997), 295–97.

40. Seligman, Martin. *Authentic Happiness* (New York: Free Press, 2002), 93–101.

41. Bragg, Rick. *I Am a Soldier, Too: The Jessica Lynch Story* (New York: Alfred A. Knopf, 2003), 120.

42. Frankl, Viktor E. *Man's Search for Meaning: An Introduction to LogoTherapy* (Boston: Beacon Press, 1959).

43. Covey, Stephen. *First Things First.*

44. Schuller, Robert. *Success is Never Ending, Failure is Never Final* (Nashville, Tennessee: Nelson Publishers, 1988).

45. Tracy, Brian. *The Excellent Manager* (Nightingale-Conant, n.d.).

46. Barron, Kenneth E. and Judith M. Harackiewicz. "Achievement Goals and Optimal Motivation: Testing Multiple Goal Models," University of Wisconsin, *Journal of Personality and Social Psychology* 80, No. 5, (2001), 706–722.

47. Brown, Les. *Live your Dreams* (New York: Morrow, 1992).

48. Shellenbarger, Sue. "On the Road Again: Parents are Spending More Time Than Ever Behind the Wheel," *Wall Street Journal*, January 30, 2003, D-1.

49. "New Study Suggests That Cell Phone Conversations Can Be a Significant Distraction for Motorists," *National Safety Council*, news release, August 16, 2001. Retrieved from http://www.nsc.org/news/nr081501a.htm.

50. Pitino, Rick. *Success is a Choice: Ten Steps to Overachieving in Business and Life* (New York: Broadway Books, 1997), 53–55.

51. King, Laura A., Jeanette H. Richards, and Emily Stemmerich. "Daily Goals, Life Goals, and Worst Fears: Means, Ends, and Subjective Well-Being," *Journal of Personality* 66, No. 5, (October 1998).

52. Covey, Stephen. *The Seven Habits of Highly Effective People* (New York: Fireside, 1989), 287.

53. Powell, Colin. *My American Journey* (New York: Ballatine Books, 1995), 28.

54. Walter, Lilly. *Secrets of Successful Speakers* (New York: McGraw-Hill, 1993), 47.

55. "The American Character," *Wall Street Journal*, March 5, 1998, A-14.

56. Gleick, James. *Chaos: Making a New Science* (New York: Viking, 1987).

57. Dyer, Wayne W. *Pulling Your Own Strings* (New York: Avon Books, 1977), 212.

58. Goleman, Daniel. *Emotional Intelligence* (New York: Bantam Books, 1995), 73.

59. "Positive Thinking Doesn't Help Cancer Patients Live Longer," *Associated Press*, October 20, 2002.

60. "Optimistic People Live Longer: But How Do You Get a Positive Attitude?," *Tufts University Health & Nutrition Letter*, (January 2003), 4.

61. Shula, Don and Ken Blanchard. *Everyone's A Coach* (Grand Rapids, Michigan: Zondervan Publishing House and Harper Business, 1995), 67.

62. Fettke, Rich. *Extreme Success* (New York: Simon and Schuster, 2002).

63. Pham, L. B. and S. E. Taylor. "From thought of action: Effects on process-versus outcome-based mental simulations on performance," *Personality and Social Psychology Bulletin* 25, (February 1999), 250–260.

64. Schultheiss, Oliver C. and Joachim C. Brunstein. "Goal imagery: Bridging the Gap Between Implicit Motives and Explicit Goals," University of Erlangen, *Journal of Personality* 67, No. 1, (February 1999), 6.

65. Buscaglia, Leo. *Loving Each Other* (New York: Ballantine, 1984).

66. Tracy, Brian. *Maximum Achievement* (New York: Simon and Schuster, 1993).

67. Walton, Mary. *The Deming Management Method* (New York: Perigee, 1986), 34–36.

68. Lakein, Alan. *How to Get Control of Your Time and Your Life* (New York: Signet Books, 1973), 96.

69. Nightingale, Earl. *Lead the Field* (Niles, IL: Nightingale-Conant, 1990), 58.

70. Butler, Gillian and Tony Hope. *Managing Your Mind* (New York: Oxford University Press, 1995), 38.

71. Kabat-Zinn, Jon. *Wherever You Go, There You Are* (New York: Hyperion, 1994), 3–7.

72. Goleman, Daniel. "Finding Happiness: Cajole Your Brain to Lean to the Left," *New York Times*, February 4, 2003. http://www.nytimes.com/2003/02/04/health/psychology/04ESSA.html?pagewanted=1&8hpib.

73. Ziglar, Zig. *Over the Top* (Nashville, Tennessee: Thomas Nelson, 1994), 18.

74. Popcorn, 169.

75. Hill, 169.

76. Covey, *The Seven Habits of Highly Effective People*, 236–60.

77. Tracy, Brian and Colin Rose. *Accelerated Learning Techniques* (New York: Simon & Schuster, 1995).

78. Klein, Frederick C. "Tiger Masters the Masters," *Wall Street Journal*, April 15, 1998.

79. Kushner, Harold S. *When All You Ever Wanted Isn't Enough: The Search for a Life That Matters* (New York: Fireside, 1986).

0-595-33147-5

www.ingramcontent.com/pod-product-compliance
Lightning Source LLC
Chambersburg PA
CBHW061357280526
45784CB00001B/291